Praying on the Edge

About Bryan Owen

Bryan Owen spent 17 years teaching English and drama including two years in Papua New Guinea as a VSO volunteer. Ordained into the ministry of the Anglican Church he has served in parishes in both Scotland and England. Having travelled widely in Eastern Europe he has specialised in Balkan affairs, human rights and the work of the United Nations. He is now pursuing an interest in helping street children in India.

Previous publications include *The Evil Eye of Gondôr*, a play for children and *Albania, Land of Eagles*, a handbook for volunteers. He is an occasional international election supervisor and he works with asylum seekers in Scotland. Married with two children he has taken early retirement from parish ministry and now writes full-time. He lives near Glasgow.

PRAYING ON THE EDGE: HUMAN RIGHTS FOR CONCERNED CHRISTIANS

Bryan Owen

Covenanters

Published by
Covenanters Press

the joint imprint of
Zeticula
57 St Vincent Crescent
Glasgow
G3 8NQ
and
Scottish Christian Press
21 Young Street
Edinburgh
EH2 4HU

http://www.covenanters.co.uk
admin@covenanters.co.uk

ISBN 1 905022 02 6 Paperback
ISBN 1 905022 03 4 Hardback

For Katy
who constantly challenges me
to look beyond myself
to all those living on the edge

GOD
WAS IN

CHRIST
RECONCILING

THE WORLD
TO HIMSELF...

ENTRUSTING TO US

THE MESSAGE OF

RECONCILIATION...
WE ARE

AMBASSADORS
FOR

CHRIST
(2 Corinthians 5:19-20)

Acknowledgements

Thank you

... to the Revd Mark Johnstone (Church of Scotland) and the Revd Robin Paisley (Scottish Episcopal Church) for their friendship, support and theological expertise;

... to friends in the Iona Community at home and abroad who are living on the edge and especially to Ellen Moxley for permission to tell her story;

... to friends and colleagues who have lived on the edge of fear and violence in Albania, Kosovo, FYR Macedonia and Serbia;

... to asylum seeker friends in London and Glasgow who have seen too much and still live in fear;

... to the street children I've met in India and West Africa and those who try to love them in so many practical ways; and

... to my former students and colleagues at Bumayong Evangelical Lutheran High School in Lae, Papua New Guinea who first opened my eyes to the dignity of those who, to our often patronising Western eyes, have so little but give so much.

Preface

We live in uncertain and unsettled times. We live with uncertainty and unsettlement in our own hearts. That is proving a trouble to many, both Christian and non-Christian, who have grown used to being settled and to being able to think forward to a future with some confidence.

Bryan Owen's life and ministry make him eminently qualified to offer us all help in coming to terms with the times we are in. This book is a different sort of guide for people and for groups. It touches the raw subjects and brings us to the Gospel along the rugged pathway of pain and conflict, anger and despair.

This book makes us all think again and think inside the life and teaching of Jesus. It draws on a rich vein of contemporary writing and reflection to assist our journeying.

For people and churches who have been disturbed by what is happening in the world and who want to respond creatively and imaginatively, this book will be an enormous help.

If it can help Christian communities to be centres of healing and reconciliation in a broken world it will have served the hidden and yet powerful life of the Kingdom Jesus brought among us.

Rt. Rev. John Gladwin
Bishop of Chelmsford
Chair, Christian Aid

Contents

Introduction

This is a book for groups. It's for believing groups and doubting groups and concerned groups and groups who are not sure where they're going. It's a book for groups that want to *do something,* for groups that want to change a bit of the world – maybe their bit of the world - for the better. It's for groups that are no longer content just to sit and talk and pray, important as that is, but for people who now want to add meaningful action to their being together.

We live in a painful world so there is much for us to do. We can do it individually or we can do it with others. We can do it denominationally or we can do it ecumenically. We can do it from within the Christian ghetto or we can do it hand in hand with those on the edge of faith and with our secular neighbours in the wider community. There is much to do and what we choose to do we do simply because we want to be faithful to Jesus. And because there is so much to do *someone's life* somewhere in this world may depend on the decision we make.

It's been said that in all ages and societies the majority of people are more attracted to the gentle than the strong and more attracted to those who suffer than to those who are successful. The instinct that moves us to compassion is generally stronger than the one that moves us to hurt or abuse or oppress those around us, although, if we are honest, we know we all have the capacity to do ill as well as good.

Jesus constantly touched on this tender spot within the human psyche in his teaching and preaching, but he also recognised the power of the fatal flaw inside us. We see it in his condemnation of the hypocrites in his own day who manipulated politics and religion for their own ends, but we also see it in the Cross and in the forgiveness of God that flows from it.

Through his own kindness and compassion Jesus reminds us that we too can be kind and compassionate even to people we don't know and from whom we expect to accrue no personal benefit. That capacity, that altruism, is God-given. We are all made in the divine image and perhaps that's why human rights historically have been so rooted in the Judaeo-Christian tradition, although cruel and barbaric events perpetrated in Europe and the Middle East in recent years may make us doubt that.

When we see people abused or oppressed by powerful despots we are outraged. When we see people going hungry or being made homeless after some terrible disaster our hearts go out to them. Our Christian understanding of things tells us that all people are loved by God and all people, therefore, have intrinsic value. We want to respond. We want to do what we know God wants to do. We want to help.

The purpose of these studies, then, is two-fold:

• Firstly, they might help us recognise there are painful situations happening in God's world that God's people can actually do something about in an effective and disciplined way. These studies are a challenge to Christian action - to incarnate the Gospel in what we know to be dark places in the world.

• Secondly, they might help us recognise painful situations in our own lives; if so, maybe God's grace can be mediated to us in more ways than we dare to hope. Maybe the other members of the group can help us and support us in this, if only we let them.

So often in our bible study groups, fellowship groups or house groups we are tempted to study or discuss mainly what helps *us* – the emphasis is on *our* faith, *our* church life, *our* relationship with God and *our* personal comfort in this life. These ten studies do include our own needs but their focus is mainly on the needs of *others*. The concern for the stranger and the oppressed is an authentic strand in biblical Christianity.

In addition to many of the Old Testament prophets who demanded justice from those in power for the poor and honest it is St John, in his first epistle, who reminds Christians that *"Those who say, 'I love God,' and hate their brothers or sisters, are liars; for those who do not love a brother or sister whom they have seen, cannot love God whom they have not seen. The commandment we have from him is this: those who love God must love their brothers and sisters also."* [1]

18

In the second part of each study the focus comes back to what we as followers of the Carpenter – either individually or in our groups - might usefully do *in response* to the situations we have studied. God loves the whole world not just our own little part of it - and God loves all people not just those who speak and think and believe and worship as we do.

St James, in his epistle, asks us this question: *"What good is it, my brothers and sisters, if you say you have faith but do not have works? Can faith save you? If a brother or sister is naked and lacks daily food, and one of you says to them, 'Go in peace; keep warm and eat your fill,' and yet you do not supply their bodily needs, what is the good of that? So faith by itself, if it has no works, is dead."*[2]

Jesus said that he came that we might have life in all its abundance.[3] Those words of promise are not just for us alone but for everyone - because all humankind is made in the divine image - not just those of us living comfortably in the Western world.

There are, broadly, two world views about the poor and the oppressed:

(i) The first says that it's not their fault, they are victims of circumstances beyond their control, they are victims of the rich and powerful, they deserve dignity in their own right, they will always exist in every society, and they should be helped and supported by those who have more – this is the view we see in the Bible and in world literature up until the 19th century; Jesus, for example, was a poor carpenter born in a stable but he had greater moral worth than Pontius Pilate, the educated imperial Roman Officer who betrayed the law and the cause of truth;

(ii) The second says that the rich and powerful are the useful ones in society not the poor, wealthy peoples' demands for fripperies and luxuries give work to the poor and they should be grateful, social progress depends on personal merit and effort; the ideology of meritocracy infers that those who are at the bottom of the pile deserve to be there because they are indolent or lacking in appropriate skills, and it's talent that merits reward; this is the view that has developed since the 18th century and finds its apogee in the culture of North

America and the so-called Protestant work ethic.[4]

Whichever view you take, Robert Runcie, when he was Archbishop of Canterbury, used to remind ordinands in his diocese that their ministry was simply *'to comfort the afflicted and to afflict the comfortable'*.[5] Perhaps, by God's good grace, this is what these studies might just help us do.

Bryan Owen
Glasgow, 2004

Leading the Group

A study group should be a place of safety for its members. It should be a place where each person is valued and loved, where their stories are heard with respect and where their views can be safely expressed even though others in the group may disagree with them. At its best, a study group can itself become a place of healing and restoration both for its members as well as for the wider world.

Gentle music in the background can help to create a welcoming atmosphere. A lighted candle in the room might symbolise the presence of Christ. If there is time why not begin the study by eating a meal together especially if you are meeting during the evening and it's a rush to get there from work?

Suggested outline for each meeting:

1. Introduction - the group might like to share news and needs before the meeting settles down with the theme and opening prayer (10-15 minutes)

2. Someone should read the theme passage out loud (10 minutes)

3. Invite members of the group to share their own experiences of or reactions to the situation - don't feel restricted by the suggested questions! (20 minutes)

4. Read the Scripture passage allowing time for reflection and response (15 minutes)

5. Faith in action: discuss how members of the group might like to respond to the issue either individually or as a group (15 minutes)

6. Closing prayers - feel free to add other prayers to those suggested including any needs expressed within the group (10 minutes)

The meeting should last about an hour and a half and could perhaps end informally with refreshments if you haven't had them earlier. In sharing experiences about the situation under discussion it's important to allow everyone who wishes to do so to speak. The more quiet and retiring members of the group should always be asked if they wish to say anything. This will help everyone to reach a deeper understanding of the situation and for the group to think about how they might actively engage with it.

These studies are intended to be both ecumenical and international in scope. Prayers are taken from Catholic, Anglican, Orthodox and Celtic traditions as well as from Jewish sources. Some come from Europe, others from India, Africa and North America.

A full list of names, addresses and contact telephone numbers for all organisations mentioned *in italics* in the studies can be found at the end of the book but be aware that details, especially websites, can change.

1

The Use of Torture

'O Lord, how long shall the wicked,
how long shall the wicked exult?'
(Psalm 94:3)

Theme

In our own country we enjoy having the freedom to express our views, to protest against wrongdoing and to demand political and social change. In many parts of the world these simple human rights are denied and those who demand them are accused of being enemies of the state. They can be imprisoned and subjected to torture often with implements made in the West.

Totalitarian regimes from Nazi Germany to the Soviet Union, from Pinochet's Chile to apartheid South Africa, have used torture as a matter of course. In the Iraq conflict in 2004, however, we discovered that some coalition soldiers, men and women who had been sent there to free the Iraqi people from tyranny, had themselves become as cruel as the interrogators of Saddam's regime they had replaced. The realisation that those who are supposed to be on the side of the good are as corruptible as the people they came to oust has shocked many people to the core.

Although the following example comes from Tibet it could come from any number of places around the world...

Opening prayer

Leader

Jesus,
you suffered the injustice of an unfair trial
and you suffered the torture of pain and humiliation -
yet you asked the Father to forgive those
who caused you such suffering:
guide us now in our thinking and speaking,
in our deciding and doing
and teach us what it is we need to learn.
Amen.

Reading

*Palden Gyatso is a Tibetan monk who was imprisoned for a total of 33
years by the Chinese authorities. In 1992 he escaped to Nepal, smuggling
with him the instruments of his torture. He now lives in Dharamsala in
India. In 1995 he testified to the UN Commission on Human Rights in
Geneva. In this extract the year is 1989 and he is incarcerated in the prison
in Drapchi.*

Suddenly the door burst open and a Tibetan guard ordered me
to go with him. He took me to an interrogation room, where I was
met by one of the old guards, whom I immediately recognised. It was
Paljor, the guard I held responsible for the death of my friend and
mentor Lobsang Wangchuk. In the old days we called Paljor 'the light
hand', because he never hesitated to raise his hand in order to beat
prisoners. He was tall and smoked constantly. His fingers were stained
yellow from the cigarettes and his eyes were watery. He was sitting
down behind a table. The two Chinese guards who had searched my
luggage stood beside the door.

Paljor was pretending to read my case file but as soon as I came in
he put the file down on the table, stood up and walked towards me,
shouting 'Rascal!' This was followed by a stream of abuse. I had no
idea what was going to happen. The interrogation room reminded me
of the shrine rooms dedicated to wrathful deities. An array of batons

24

hung on the wall. A bunch of shining steel handcuffs dangled from a hook. Paljor took down a long baton and walked around me, waving it in the air.

'You've been thrown in prison three times and still you have failed to reform,' he said.

He began questioning me about my past offences, even though he must have known all about my case history from my file.

'How old are you?' he asked.

'Sixty.'

'No! You are fifty-nine!' Paljor was clearly trying to provoke me.

'I was born in the year of the monkey, and that makes me sixty.'

Paljor had moved back to the rack of batons. He selected a shorter one, about a foot long, and pushed it into an electric socket to recharge it. Sparks shot out and there was a crackling sound.

'Why are you here?' continued Paljor.

'Because I put up posters in Lhasa calling for Tibetan independence.'

'So you still want Rangsten?' he asked, still trying to provoke me.

Paljor did not wait for me to answer. He pulled the electric baton from the socket and began to poke me with this new toy. My whole body flinched at each electric shock. Then, shouting obscenities, he thrust the baton into my mouth, took it out, then rammed it in again. Paljor went back to the wall and selected a longer baton. I felt as though my body were being torn apart. I remember dimly that one of the guards put his fingers in my mouth to pull out my tongue and prevent me from choking. And I remember too that one of the Chinese guards ran out of the room in disgust.

I can remember as if it were yesterday the way the shocks made my body vibrate. The shock seemed to hold you in its grip, like a furious shiver. I passed out and when I woke I found myself lying in a pool of vomit and urine. I had no idea how long I had been there. My mouth was swollen and I could hardly move my jaw. With great pain, I spat something out. It was three of my own teeth. It would be several weeks before I could eat solid food again. In due course, all my other teeth fell out too.

I was taken back to the dormitory. Yeshe was there.
'Who did this?' he asked me.
'Paljor,' I mumbled, as Yeshe helped me on to the bed.
(from 'Fire Under the Snow' by Palden Gyatso pp194-196)

Sharing our own experiences

1. Are you emotionally and spiritually moved when you hear of such suffering? How do you want to respond?

2. Have you ever suffered physical, emotional or mental torture in your own life – at school, at work, in your neighbourhood or at home?

3. Do you think you have imposed suffering or stress on others no matter how unintentionally?

Scripture reading

John 19:1-16

In these verses describing the crucifixion we are reminded that Jesus was given an unjust trial (v6), and he suffered verbal humiliation (v3) and physical abuse (v2) before his execution. In the Passion Christ identifies with the heart of the human condition: the pain and suffering that are the consequence of our estrangement from the God who created us in such love. Jesus was an innocent man being put to death in order to protect the corrupt and unjust from any further challenges.

Faith sharing

1. In your own lives are you ever tempted to ignore Christian precepts about honesty and truth?

2. Are there times when you feel estranged from God? Do you ever feel the absence of God and, like Jesus, cry out *'My God, my God, why have you forsaken me?'*[6] If so, how do you cope when that happens?

3. The Crucifixion was followed by the Resurrection. Do you find any comfort in that when you are going through difficult times?

Action

1. Write to *Amnesty International* for information on the work they do. Consider being a supporter and perhaps join a local Amnesty group. Write letters of support on behalf of Amnesty International's prisoners of conscience.

2. Write to the *Free Tibet Campaign* or *Action of Christians Against Torture (ACAT-UK)* and consider supporting their work.

3. Write a polite letter to the *Premier of China* with a copy to the *Chinese Ambassador* in London expressing your concern about the continuing treatment of Tibetans by the Chinese authorities.[7]

Some books for further reading

Fire Under the Snow by Palden Gyatso, published by Vintage 1998, *ISBN 1-86046-509-9*
Heroes by John Pilger, published by Pan Books *1989*, *ISBN 0-330-31064-X*
The Power and the Glory by Graham Greene, published by Penguin 2003, *ISBN 0-142-43730-1*
Audacity to Believe by Sheila Cassidy, published by Darton, Longman & Todd 1992, *ISBN 0-232-51987-0*

*

Postscript

APPEAL

'We appeal to you to come forward in your multitude
and let your roar of support
echo along the path of truth and justice and decency.
Help to deliver us.
Help us to be free, to be independent,
to be able to do what we choose - in our own country.'
(Palden Gyatso - ex-political prisoner)

*

ELECTRO SHOCK BATONS

Made in Britain. Sold by Britain.
Voltage: 160,000 or 200,000
Features: finger trigger mechanism
3-5 second delivery for temporary paralysis
Available with holster
Immediate effects include severe pain, loss of muscle control,
convulsions, fainting and involuntary defecation. Longer term effects
include impotence, post-traumatic stress disorder, severe depression,
chronic anxiety and memory loss
(source: Amnesty International)

*

Closing worship

In your prayers remember
* all those in prison who are suffering torture and other cruel or inhuman punishments
* torturers and the systems that spawn them
* Amnesty International and all who work on behalf of prisoners of conscience
* all those who administer justice

Leader

O God, hasten the day when all men and women may
live with justice and dignity, freedom and peace, as
we look for the coming of his kingdom among us in
righteousness and truth; this we pray in the name of
the King of Peace, even Jesus Christ our Lord.
Amen.

All

**God the Father, bless us and our loved ones
God the Son, bless all those who suffer cruel
and inhuman punishments
God the Holy Spirit, bless the world with new
and liberating life;
Father, Son and Holy Spirit, bless us all that
we in our turn may become a blessing to one
another and to you.
Amen.**

2

Dark Times

'The light shines in the darkness, and the darkness did not overcome it.'
(John 1:5)

Theme

There are times when most of us go through what St John of the Cross calls 'the dark night of the soul'. Everything seems to be against us and our faith in God is tested to its limits. But sometimes it's when we are most alone that we find God does not fail us. When we are travelling through the dark times, painful as they might be, it's then we can discover that God is there with us all the time.

Opening prayer

Leader

Lord, our God, whose might is beyond compare and whose glory is beyond understanding, whose mercy is without measure and whose love for mankind is beyond all telling, look upon us and upon this home/ place, Master, according to your loving kindness, and bestow on us as we share together your acts of rich mercy and compassion. For to you belong all glory, honour and worship, to the Father, the Son and the Holy Spirit, now and for ever, and to the end of ages. **Amen.**

(Prayer of the First Antiphon of the Orthodox Liturgy of St John Chrysostom, adapted)

Reading

In 1991 the Albanian communist government collapsed. In the autumn of that year the country was opened up to Western aid. Bryan Owen and Dr Duncan McIntyre FRCP were among the first to take emergency supplies to a country that had been closed to Westerners since before 1967.

Ana and Gjinofeva were saying their prayers. It was a Sunday morning in November 1991. My medical colleague Duncan McIntyre and I had been in Albania for nearly a week but the hospital stores were closed for the day. Maksim, our interpreter, said he would take us to Durrës on the coast where we could swim and relax. His son Taulant came with us.

'Come,' Maksim said, 'we'll show you one of our ancient ruins.'

We got out of the car and followed Maksim up a track and there before us were the remains of a 2nd century Roman amphitheatre. The place was overgrown and unkempt but, we were told, was listed as a UNESCO heritage site.

We went down some steps into the catacombs and found ourselves in a ruined Byzantine chapel with the remains of some frescos on the walls. Ana and Gjinofeva, two elderly ladies dressed in black, had lit some candles on the remains of the altar and had placed two painted eggs beneath. As we entered they looked up fearfully.

With Taulant translating we introduced ourselves as aid workers from Scotland. I wasn't wearing clerical uniform that day but Taulant explained to them that I was a priest. Their faces lit up. They were Orthodox and their priest had disappeared in the religious purges of 1967. Since then they had faithfully crept down to this ancient chapel to say their prayers secretly in the country that styled itself as the world's first atheistic state. The practice of religion, even in private, had been outlawed. Most churches and mosques had either been destroyed or turned to some other use. Few survived.

We were moved by their story and by their courage. Had they been caught they would have faced imprisonment or even death. Their faith and their continued faithfulness in spite of all the dangers they had faced put me to shame. But somehow Ana and Gjinofeva were saying something quite profound it seemed to me. Here they were in a ruined chapel under a ruined amphitheatre in a ruined country keeping the flickering flame of faith alight. They were holding on to Christian hope when for others all hope had been trampled on and destroyed by the apparatchiks of Enver Hoxha's Party of Labour - the communists. In the autumn of 1991, however, the communists were still the party of government and its supporters were fighting a rearguard action in the country to preserve their powerbase. We still had to be careful.

Ana and Gjinofeva gave me one of their painted eggs - the Orthodox symbol of the Risen Christ - to take away with me. I asked them if they would like me to say a prayer for them and with Taulant translating (who was from a Muslim background!) I pronounced the General Absolution and gave them God's blessing - the first time they had heard such words in twenty-four years.

I am an Anglican priest and as such I'm not recognised by the Orthodox churches as being a validly ordained minister. But here I was in Durrës with two Christian believers who desperately needed to hear God's words of forgiveness and love and for the first time in a quarter of a century they received the assurance of his blessing. I often wonder what God thinks about all our theological wrestling. In this one moment heaven and earth met and we were flooded with the love of the one God we all worshipped. I had tears in my eyes as we said our farewells.

Many of the missionary groups that invaded the country in those heady months after 1991 went to 'take Christ to Albania'. Ana and Gjinofeva taught me that Christ had never left. He had been there all those years with his suffering people. Within the ruins where once Christians had been thrown to the lions there was still hope and the Faith had been kept alive.

(Bryan Owen)

Sharing our own experiences

1. Are you aware of any Christians today being persecuted for their faith?

2. What experience do you have of committed atheists? Do they respect your beliefs? Do you respect theirs?

3. Are you or any members of your family ridiculed for being practising Christians?

Scripture reading

2 Corinthians 1:1-11

Paul had been under a great deal of pressure for some time and had suffered even to the point where he and his companions had felt *'utterly, unbearably, crushed that we despaired of life itself'* (v8). And yet, in spite of this, his faith in God helped him cope and survive.

In his own suffering Paul identifies with Christ's suffering on the Cross but being 'in Christ' he also shares in Christ's comfort and strength. Therefore, he says, all Christians can share in the comfort and hope that God gives whatever it is that they're suffering.

Paul's hope had been set on the One who rose from the dead (v9) and he believes that the One in whom he believes will continue to rescue him in the days to come (v10). Whatever the sufferings of this present world he says that the power of the resurrection will ultimately triumph.

Faith sharing

1. What pressures have tempted you to give up your faith? How did you respond to them?

2. What has been your experience of God's comfort in your own adversities?

3. What do you believe is the place of prayer on behalf of others? In what way can it be *effective*?

Action

1. Write to *Christian Solidarity International* or *The Barnabas Fund* for information on the work they do on behalf of Christians who are persecuted for their faith. Consider being a supporter.

2. Write to your MP or to the appropriate ambassador on behalf of any individual or group suffering simply because they hold to the Christian faith.

3. Write to *Amnesty International* to see if there is someone you could regularly pray for.

Some books for further reading

Darkness at Noon by Arthur Koestler, published by Vintage Books 1994, *ISBN 0-09-942491-6*

Nineteen-eighty-four by George Orwell, published by Penguin Books 1990, *ISBN 0-1401-2671-6*

Dark Night of the Soul by St John of the Cross, published by Dover Publications 2003, *ISBN 0-486-42693-9*

Windows onto God by Robert Runcie, published by SPCK 1983, *ISBN 0-281-04076-1*

*

Postscript

THE FLICKERING FLAME

Even in
the dark night of peoples,
there are those
who keep alive
the flickering flame.
From humble prayer,
they draw the freedom
to resist harsh turmoil,
their souls lifted high
with hope.
(Brother Roger of the Taizé Community)

*

I AM

I am! yet what I am none cares or knows?
My friends forsake me like a memory lost.
I am the self-consumer of my woes;
They rise and vanish, an oblivious host,
Shadows of life, whose very soul is lost.
And yet I am – I live – though I am toss'd.
(John Clare 1793-1864, English poet)

*

LIVING WITH THE QUESTIONS

Be patient toward all that is unsolved
in your heart...
Try to love the questions themselves.

Do not now seek the answers,
which cannot be given
because you would not be able
to live them.
And the point is,
to live everything.

Live the questions now.
Perhaps you will then
gradually,
without noticing it,
live along some distant day
into the answers.
*(Rainer Marie Rilke 1875-1926, Austrian writer,
in 'Letters to a Young Poet')*

*

AFFIRMATION

A woman in great distress over the death of her son
came to the Master for comfort.

He listened to her patiently
while she poured out her tale of woe.

Then he said softly,
'I cannot wipe away your tears, my dear.
I can only teach you how to make them holy.'
(Anthony de Mello SJ, d. 1987, Indian Jesuit writer)

Closing worship

In your prayers remember
* Christians who suffer for their faith
* those in our own country who feel ridiculed because of their
faith
* those who are going through dark times in their relationship
with God

Leader

In peace, let us pray to the Lord
All   **Lord, have mercy**

For the peace from above, and for the salvation of our
souls
Lord, have mercy

For the peace of the whole world, for the welfare of
the holy churches of God, and for the union of all, let
us pray to the Lord
Lord, have mercy

For our church/churches, and for those who enter
with faith, devotion and fear of God, let us pray to the
Lord
Lord, have mercy

For our church leaders, for all clergy and people, let us
pray to the Lord
Lord, have mercy

For our country, for all civil authorities, and for all
who exercise responsibility in our society, let us pray
to the Lord
Lord, have mercy

For ourselves, for our loved ones, for our faith with all its uncertainties, let us pray to the Lord
Lord, have mercy

Lord, as we depart, give us your blessing
Amen

(from the 'Litany of Peace' of the Orthodox Liturgy of St John Chrysostom, adapted)

All

May the blessing of the Lord and his mercy be upon us through his grace and love for humankind, always, now and ever and unto ages of ages.
Amen.

(blessing from the Orthodox liturgy, adapted)

3

Freedom from Fear

'Never let the oil of the wicked anoint my head,
for my prayer is continually against their wicked deeds.'

(Psalm 141:5)

Theme

Many people around the world live in fear. They are afraid of the early morning knock on the door, or being bundled into a car as they walk on the street. They are afraid of the trumped up charge or the assassin's bullet. If they speak out in places like Zimbabwe or North Korea or Uzbekistan as others used to speak out in the former Soviet Union or East Germany they know what the consequences might be. So they huddle in fear in their homes, afraid of the knock on the door. In Iraq and Palestine and Chechnya they know they are powerless to make things better.

One example of non-violent protest is Daw Aung San Suu Kyi (pronounced *chee*)[8]. She is a human rights activist, Nobel Prize laureate and the leader of Burma's National League for Democracy. In 1990 her party won an overwhelming victory at the polls but the Burmese military authorities refused to hand over power. Since then she has been frequently kept under house arrest in Rangoon.[9] Her movements are severely restricted, her phone line is frequently cut and she has been prevented from seeing her family in England.

Even though she could choose a safe and comfortable life in exile in the West Daw Suu remains a defiant symbol of hope for the people of Burma, a country described by a BBC correspondent as *'one vast labour camp'*.

Opening prayer

Leader

> O Thou who hast given us eyes
> to see the light that fills this room,
> give us the inward vision
> to behold thee in this place -
> in our listening,
> in our speaking
> and in our love for one another.
> **Amen.**

(from India, adapted)

Reading

Burma, a country of 47 million people, is ruled by fear. A military machine of 400,000 soldiers denies a whole nation its most basic rights. Burma, a country of intense natural beauty, is governed by one of the most brutal and corrupt regimes in the world:

* over two million people - men, women and children work in forced labour
* there are one and a half million refugees within Burma's borders
* 250,000 minority Muslim Rohingya refugees fled to Bangladesh in 1991
* 110,000 minority Karen and Mon refugees fled to Thailand in 1994
* there are around 1,500 political prisoners in the country
* Burma is the world's largest producer of illegal opium

Daw Suu's political party, the National League for Democracy (the NLD) won 82% of the seats in the 1990 general election when the people of Burma overwhelmingly rejected military rule. The military then simply refused to recognise the result and hand over power to the newly elected leaders. The NLD, ethnic minorities, students and monks continue to resist the regime despite a highly repressive political environment.

The junta allows no freedom of expression. Publications are censored, there is a 20 year prison sentence for anyone opposing the junta's policies and there is a 15 year prison sentence for anyone found in possession of a fax machine or computer modem. Members of the NLD are constantly harassed, threatened, arrested and tortured. The regime demands that the Buddhist clergy support its rule and troops regularly invade monasteries to remove Buddhist leaders who support human rights. Muslim and Christian minority leaders are also targets for army attacks.

The regime is desperate for foreign currency with military spending absorbing an estimated 40% of public sector spending. The armed forces number 400,0000 in a country which has had no external aggressors since independence in 1948.

In order to generate hard currency the regime is now promoting Burma as a new and exotic holiday destination. Some people argue that increased tourism will open the country to liberalising forces but the reverse seems to be true.

Tourists find it difficult to meet ordinary Burmese and tourism profits rarely reach ordinary people. The army itself is a partner in many joint tourist ventures with foreign companies and so profits go to the military. It is believed that many hotel projects are fronts for laundering money from Burma's heroin trade.

Large-scale forced labour has been reported throughout Burma with the army conscripting people to build roads, railways, hotels and other tourist infrastructure. A Thai journalist reported seeing *young boys of 13 or 14 chained and working - some had their legs bandaged where the manacles have rubbed their skin raw'.*

A Financial Times journalist writing in 1995 said, *'I saw prisoners in leg irons begging by the roadside in the southeast, and thousands of prisoners and 'volunteers' cleaning the Royal Palace Moat in Mandalay, with little more than their bare hands...'*

One Karen refugee said *'They took us on trucks, 50 of us at a time... We had to work in chains, we had to carry rocks, and whenever we weren't quick enough or if the rocks were too heavy for us to carry, we were hit with a bamboo stick. They beat me so hard with it sometimes that I just wanted to die... some men were unconscious, then they were left lying there the whole day like that. In front of my own eyes I saw two old men beaten to death.'*

In all cases of forced labour people are required to provide their own tools and food. Often the villagers are working on land which once belonged to them but has been taken from them with no compensation.

In cases where the work site is far from their village, people have to sleep by the side of the road or railway they are building with no shelter or sanitary facilities. Amnesty International reports cases of women who are forced to stay overnight being raped by army officers. Refugees report severe beatings of conscripts whose work does not satisfy the soldiers. There is constant malnutrition in the forced labour camps with deaths among the elderly and children being high.

The Burmese junta is committing human rights abuses such as forced labour and forced relocation on a wide scale throughout the country. The people of Burma long for the freedoms we all take for granted: freedom to make their own choices, freedom to express their opinions, freedom to live and work in peace. They long for freedom from fear itself. All their hopes are pinned on Daw Aung San Suu Kyi imprisoned in her house on University Avenue - the one person the junta are afraid to touch.

(sources: Burma Campaign UK and the Burma Project USA)

*

Sharing our own experiences

1. What are your immediate feelings in response to what you have heard?

2. Countries like Israel/Palestine, Zimbabwe and Burma are a long way away. Is it our responsibility to get involved?

3. Have you ever felt as if you were not in control of your own circumstances?

Scripture reading

Luke 1:46-56

Mary's Song, the *Magnificat*, is so radical it could almost be mistaken for the manifesto of a political or social revolution. It begins with Mary's praise of God - *My soul magnifies the Lord* (v46) but what follows is based on the Song of Hannah in I Samuel 2:1-10. Mary says that as she has been exalted from her low degree so the poor and oppressed will be released from their suffering in God's new order – the kingdom which has already begun.

For generations the cutting edge of the Magnificat has been obscured by the beautiful way it was sung in traditional Evensong. Perhaps now that new liturgies are being used we should release Mary's song to galvanise Christian people once again so that they can become *signs* of the new kingdom that Christ, Mary's Son, came to proclaim.

Christ has no hands but our hands, no feet but our feet and no voice but our voice. God works his will through us, weak and imperfect as we are. A modern story tells of the man who was praying to God asking him why he hadn't won the lottery. 'Tell me, God, why you haven't answered my prayer?' he said. Day after day the man prayed thus until in exasperation God replied. 'Okay. Let's meet halfway. *Go and buy a ticket first.*'

If God is to scatter the proud and put down the mighty from their thrones, if he is to exalt those of low degree and fill the hungry with good things then he does it *through* those of us who are willing to respond to his call to action. We have to do our part. Sitting on our hands waiting for others to do something is not an option.

Faith sharing

1. What in the Magnificat speaks to you most strongly?

2. Why do you think the radicalism of the words has failed to move so many Christians to action?

3. If you composed *your* song what would it say?

Faith in Action

1. Write to the *Burma Campaign UK* for further information. Consider becoming a supporter.

2. Write a polite letter to the *Burmese (Myanmar) Embassy* or to *H.E. The Minister for Hotels and Tourism, Ministry of Hotels and Tourism, 77/91 Sule Pagoda Road, Rangoon, Burma (Fax +95-1-89588)* expressing your concerns.

3. Write a letter of support and encouragement to *Daw Aung San Suu Kyi at 54/56 University Road, Rangoon, Burma*

4. Contact *Amnesty International* for further information on prisoners of conscience in Burma.

5. Contact the *www.freeburmacoalition.org* or *www.freeburma.org* websites for further information or go to *www.dassk.com* for more information about Daw Aung San Suu Kyi herself.

*

Some books for further reading

Freedom from Fear by Aung San Suu Kyi, published by Penguin 1991, *ISBN 0-14-017089-8*

The Voice of Hope conversations with Aung San Suu Kyi, published by Penguin 1997, *ISBN 1-5706-2410-0*

The Lady an autobiography by Aung San Suu Kyi, published by Faber & Faber 1998 *ISBN 0-571-19944-5*

Blood Brothers by Elias Chacour, published by Chosen Books 1987 *ISBN 0-310-60810-4*

The Heart Must Break by James Mawdsley, published by Arrow 2002 *ISBN 0-09-942694-3*

Postscript

THE 1991 NOBEL PEACE PRIZE

On 14 October 1991 Aung San Suu Kyi was awarded the 1991 Nobel Peace Prize. This is the Press Release recognising Suu's work on behalf of the people of Burma.

'The Norwegian Nobel Committee has decided to award the Nobel Peace Prize for 1991 to Aung San Suu Kyi of Burma for her non-violent struggle for democracy and human rights.

Aung San Suu Kyi is the daughter of Burma's liberation leader Aung San and showed an early interest in Ghandi's philosophy of non-violent protest. After having refrained from political activity, she became involved in 'the second struggle for national independence' in Burma in 1988. She became the leader of a democratic opposition which employs non-violent means to resist a regime characterised by brutality. She also emphasises the need for conciliation between the sharply divided regions and ethnic groups in her country.

The election held in May 1990 resulted in a conclusive victory for the opposition. The regime ignored the election results; Suu Kyi refused to leave the country, and since then she has been kept under strict house arrest. Suu Kyi's struggle is one of the most extraordinary examples of civil courage in Asia in recent decades. She has become an important symbol in the struggle against oppression.

In awarding the Nobel Peace Prize for 1991 to Aung San Suu Kyi, the Norwegian Nobel Committee wishes to honour this woman for her unflagging efforts and to show its support for the many people throughout the world who are striving to attain democracy, human rights and ethnic conciliation by peaceful means.'

*

WOMEN DON'T START WARS

In a speech to her supporters in 1995 Aung San Suu Kyi said, "…to the best of my knowledge, no war was ever started by women. But it is women and children who have always suffered the most in situations of conflict.

"There is an outmoded Burmese proverb still recited by men, who wish to deny that women too can play a part in bringing necessary change and progress to their society: 'The dawn rises only when the rooster crows.' But Burmese people today are well aware of the scientific reason behind the rising of dawn and the falling of dusk. And the intelligent rooster surely realizes that it is because dawn comes that it crows and not the other way around.

"It crows to welcome the light that has come to relieve the darkness of night. It is not the prerogative of men alone to bring light to the world: women with their capacity for compassion and self-sacrifice, their courage and perseverance, have done much to dissipate the darkness of intolerance and hate, suffering and despair."

(Aung San Suu Kyi, 1995)

*

IN THE QUIET LAND
by Aung San Suu Kyi, 2003

In the Quiet Land, no one can tell
if there's someone who's listening
for secrets they can sell.
The informers are paid in the blood of the land
and no one dares speak what the tyrants won't stand.
In the quiet land of Burma,
no one laughs and no one thinks out loud.
In the quiet land of Burma,
you can hear it in the silence of the crowd
In the Quiet Land, no one can say
when the soldiers are coming
to carry them away.
The Chinese want a road; the French want the oil;
the Thais take the timber; and SLORC takes the spoils...
In the Quiet Land....
In the Quiet Land, no one can hear
what is silenced by murder
and covered up with fear.
But, despite what is forced, freedom's a sound
that liars can't fake and no shouting can drown.

*

A PLEA
'Please use your liberty
to promote ours'
(Aung San Suu Kyi)

*

Closing worship

In your prayers remember
* Aung San Suu Kyi under house arrest and all members of the pro-democracy movement in Burma
* the State Law and Order Restoration Council (the military government)
* the United Nations and all who might bring pressure for change

Leader

> Almighty God, creator of the universe, source of love, wisdom and truth, make us instruments of your perfect will. Bless the United Nations, and all those who speak in its Councils, and carry out its work for international understanding, the restraining of violence, and the promotion of justice and peace; and may all peoples of your world be brought into that unity which accords with your perfect will.
> **Amen.**

All

> **The Lord bless us and keep us, the Lord make his face to shine upon us and be gracious unto us, the Lord look kindly upon us and give us his blessing of peace, this day/night and for evermore.**
> **Amen.**

4

The Power of Friendship

'A friend loves at all times'
(Proverbs 17:17)

Theme

We all need friends - people we feel comfortable with, people with whom we can spend time and share our thoughts. Sometimes friendship is forged in difficult circumstances. At other times friendship comes upon us unexpectedly.

Most of us have acquaintances, colleagues at work, neighbours we chat to. But who do we really trust with our deepest thoughts and our most desperate needs? How many people can we really call our friends? And how many people regard us as their friend – someone who is trustworthy and utterly reliable at all times?

Opening prayer

Leader

Jesus, you no longer call us servants but friends:
strengthen our friendship one with another, help us
to be good friends to those whose friendship we have
long valued and assure us of your continued friendship
in our own lives; this we pray for your own Name's
sake.
Amen.

Story

Brian Keenan and John McCarthy were imprisoned in the Lebanon for 5 years by religious fundamentalists. On one occasion Brian Keenan had severe diarrhoea and stomach cramps. In this extract he describes how John McCarthy selflessly cared for him.

For almost two weeks I could not eat and suffered the pain and indignity of the plastic bag and living through the stink of it until the morning, when I would take it to the toilet, wash it and return with it. John suffered too, knowing my pain and my total exhaustion. I raged at God for not ending this suffering. I could not endure this constant emptying of myself into a bag, followed by vomiting. I drank, and it came through my bowels. I thought my urine had redirected itself. I had neither the energy nor the will to make that quick dive to the corner and get my shorts around my ankles and place that bag strategically.

On many occasions it came out of me before I could reach the bag. When I did try to eat, the solid food ran from me and over me and onto my mattress. Lying exhausted, with an agonised embarrassment I watched my friend clean the mess off me without complaint. He was a very proper nurse, diligent in his work and tender in his passion, never once complaining of the filth he had to dip his hands into and never once complaining of being constantly wakened in the night by my retching and by my bowels exploding.

I often thought how having to live beside a man so ill and watch his illness and his helplessness is almost as bad for those who watch as those who suffer... It was the longest illness I had ever known. Weight fell from me. My legs were like needles; all the muscle tone that I had spent so long building up was gone.

John's unremitting ministrations revealed another side of him to me. The buffoon, the fool, the comic was a man of vast tenderness, a man of compassion... Through the mangle I went, and was stretched and pulled. I believed John thought I was sleeping, then I felt his hand lie gently on my stomach, and it remained there. He was praying. I was overcome. I was lost for words again. I wanted to join him in prayer, I wanted to thank him for this huge and tender gesture. It revealed more courage than my battling with the guards.

(from 'An Evil Cradling' by Brian Keenan, pp 249-251)

Sharing our own experiences

1. Have you ever had to care for someone who was seriously ill? What did it mean for you? And what do you think it meant for the person you were caring for?

2. Have you ever been treated unjustly? How did you feel when it happened? How do you feel now? Did you 'rage' against God?

3. What is it that you value most in your friendships?

Scripture reading

John 15:12-17

These verses remind us that at the heart of the Christian faith is unconditional and self-sacrificing love. That is the quality of Christ's love for us. Verse 13 is often found engraved on the tombstones of members of the armed forces who gave their lives in war. They gave the ultimate sacrifice by laying down their lives for their friends and country.

Jesus encourages his disciples that he chose them – he chose you and me - to go and bear fruit in the world. We are, therefore, to love each other with that same quality of sacrificial love with which Christ loves us. If we - the disciples of Jesus today - do that he tells us that we shall *'bear fruit that will last'* (v16) and the world will then become a much better place. Love is better than hatred or suspicion – yet love, practical, unconditional love, often seems in such short supply – even in our church congregations let alone in the secular world.

Faith sharing

1. Can you think of a time when a friend helped you through a crisis? What happened?

2. Jesus calls us *his friends*. What do you think that means?

3. What *fruit* do you think Christians might bear if they were to love one another as Christ loves us?

Faith in Action

1. Consider how you may offer your friendship beyond your present circle of friends. Are you able or willing to offer the kind of love and compassion Brian Keenan saw in John McCarthy?

2. Write to your local *Social Services* office to see if there's any way you might be able to care for people near where you live, or to your *Local Authority* to see if they are looking for volunteers to help with voluntary groups.

3. Could you consider being a *pastoral assistant or visitor* in your local church?

4. Could you pray regularly for an individual or group who have been taken hostage somewhere in the world?

Some books for further reading

An Evil Cradling by Brian Keenan, published by Vintage 1993, *ISBN 0-09-999030-X*
Some Other Rainbow by John McCarthy and Jill Morrell, published 1994, *ISBN 0-5521-3953-X*
Taken on Trust by Terry Waite, published 1994, *ISBN 0-340-60969-9*
Charlotte Gray by Sebastian Faulks, published by Vintage 1999, *ISBN 0-09-939431-6*

Postscript

AN OLD HASIDIC TALE

The rabbi asked his students: "How can we determine the hour of dawn, when the night ends and the day begins?"

One of the rabbi's students suggested: "When from a distance you can distinguish between a dog and a sheep?"

"No," was the answer of the rabbi.

"Is it when one can distinguish between a fig tree and a grapevine?" asked a second student.

"No," the rabbi said.

"Please tell us the answer, then," said the students.

"It is, then," said the wise teacher, "when you can look into the face of human beings and you have enough light within you to recognise them as your brothers and sisters. Up until then it is night, and darkness is still with us."

*

WHAT IS REAL?

"What is REAL?" asked the Rabbit one day when they were lying side by side near the nursery fender one day... "Does it mean having things that buzz inside you and a stick-out handle?"

"Real isn't how you are made," said the Skin Horse. "It's a thing that happens to you. When a child loves you for a long, long time, not just to play with, but REALLY loves you, then you become Real."

"Does it hurt?" asked the Rabbit.

"Sometimes," said the Skin Horse, for he was always truthful. "When you are Real you don't mind being hurt."

"Does it happen all at once, like being wound up," he asked, "or bit by bit?"

"It doesn't happen all at once," said the Skin Horse. "You become. It takes a long time. That's why it doesn't happen often to people who break easily, or have sharp edges, or who have to be carefully kept. Generally, by the time you are Real, most of your hair has been loved off, and your eyes drop out and you get all loose in the joints and very shabby. But these things don't matter at all, because once you are Real you can't be ugly, except to people who don't understand."

(from 'The Velveteen Rabbit' by Margery Williams)

*

WEEPING TOGETHER

Eat and drink together
talk and laugh together,
enjoy life together;
but never call it friendship
until we have wept together.
(traditional African saying)

*

Closing worship

In your prayers remember
* your friends
* the lonely and isolated
* those unlawfully held captive in many different parts of
the world

Leader

> Come, Lord Jesus,
> to all whose life is empty
> or for whom life is over-busy;
> give meaning and purpose
> to those whose life seems pointless
> or intolerable;
> when relationships are hurtful
> and love is not returned
> bring your healing;
> and to those who cause suffering
> bring repentance and new life.
> Come, Lord Jesus, come.
> **Amen.**

| Leader | Lord strengthen every good |
| **All** | **Defeat the power of evil** |

Lord strengthen every light
Defeat the power of darkness

Lord strengthen every power
Defeat the power of weakness

Lord strengthen every joy
Defeat the power of sadness

Lord strengthen every love
Defeat the power of hatred

Lord strengthen every life
Defeat the power of death.

Amen.

(David Adam)

5

Forgiveness and Reconciliation

'Forgive us our sins as we forgive those who sin against us.'
(Matthew 6:12 – Anglican Book of Common Worship)

Theme

We all hurt other people from time to time through our own selfish actions. However, in some parts of the world the hurt caused is so oppressive and cruel it's difficult to see how it can be forgiven and the parties reconciled. That may be true, for example, in parts of Northern Ireland, Israel/Palestine and some of the Balkan and Caucasian countries – places where there have been long-standing grievances and hatred. However, in South Africa the process of reconciliation and forgiveness began when President Nelson Mandela set up the Truth & Reconciliation Commission under the chairmanship of Archbishop Desmond Tutu...

Opening prayer

Leader

Lord, as we gather, let us dream. Let us prophesy. Let us see visions of love, peace and justice. Let us affirm with humility, with joy, with faith, with courage and in confidence that you, O Christ, are the life of the world.
Amen.

(from South Africa)

Reading

On 27 April 1994 South Africa held its first multiracial election. Shortly afterwards the Truth and Reconciliation Commission travelled the country hearing the stories of those who had suffered under apartheid.

In September 1992, what came to be known as the Bisho massacre happened. Bisho was in the Eastern Cape, the capital of the 'independent' homeland of Ciskei, ruled by Brigadier Oupa Gqozo. At first he was friendly towards the ANC but relations soured especially when he decreed Ciskei a virtual no-go area for the party. The ANC decided to stage a march on Bisho to highlight its campaign for free political activity in all the homelands and particularly Ciskei, Bophuthatswana and KwaZulu... Thirty people died as a result. When the ANC marched for free political activity, Ciskeian Defence Force soldiers fired on unarmed demonstrators. Twenty-eight protestors died in the immediate aftermath of the shootings, together with a CDF soldier shot by his colleagues. Another ANC supporter died in 1995 from his injuries.

The Commission held two hearings on the Bisho massacre, the first of which took place in Bisho itself, not far from where it had happened. The hall in which we met was packed to the rafters with those who had either been injured in the incident or who had lost loved ones, as well as those who had participated in the doomed march. The tension in the room was palpable... One of the first witnesses was the former head of the Ciskeian Defence Force, Major-General Marius Oelschig. He incensed the audience perhaps not so much by what he said as by how he said it. It may have been that he was carrying himself as a soldier, with his feelings very much under control. This may be how soldiers should conduct themselves, not carrying their hearts on their sleeves, but when people have been traumatised and their feelings are raw then such an attitude comes across as hard, unsympathetic and cynical. The temperature went up a few degrees by the time he finished testifying.

The next witnesses were former CDF officers, one white and the others black. The white officer, Colonel Horst Schobesberger, was their spokesperson. He said that it was true that they had given the orders for the soldiers to open fire. The tension in the hall became so thick that, as they say, you could have cut it with a knife. The audience could not have been more hostile. Then he turned towards the audience and made an extraordinary appeal:

> *'I say we are sorry. I say the burden of the Bisho Massacre will be on our shoulders for the rest of our lives. We cannot wish it away. It happened. But please, I ask specifically the victims not to forget - I cannot ask this - but to forgive us, to get the soldiers back into the community, to accept them fully, to try to understand also the pressure they were under then. This is all I can do. I'm sorry, this I can say, I'm sorry.'*

That crowd, which had been close to lynching them, did something quite unexpected. It broke out into thunderous applause - unbelievable. The mood change was startling. The Colonel's colleagues joined him in apologising and when the applause died down I said:

> *'Can we just keep a moment's silence because we are dealing with things that are very, very deep. It isn't easy as we all know to ask for forgiveness and it's also not easy to forgive, but we are people who know that when someone cannot be forgiven there is no future. If a husband and wife quarrel and they don't one of them say "I am sorry" and the other says "I forgive", the relationship is in jeopardy. We have been given an example by our president and by many other people.'*

No one could have predicted that day's turn of events at the hearing. It was as if someone had waved a special magic wand which transformed anger and tension into this remarkable display of communal forgiveness and acceptance of erstwhile perpetrators. We could only be humbled by it all, and deeply thankful that so-called ordinary people could be so generous and gracious.

(from 'No Future Without Forgiveness' by Desmond Tutu pp 115-117)

Sharing our own experiences

1. Are there situations in your own life where you find it hard to forgive or be forgiven?

2. Can you describe any moments of reconciliation in your life? How did you feel about them?

3. Is there someone you are estranged from but with whom you would like to be reconciled if only it could happen?

Scripture reading

Matthew 18:15-22

In these verses Jesus reminds us of the importance of admitting our faults and putting things right. He even offers a process whereby that can happen (vv15-17) but how practical do you think it is? Could it happen in your church?

Jesus then says that in the Kingdom of Heaven which is now dawning we must nurture a spirit of forgiveness rather than harbour resentment and bitterness against those who hurt us. How many times should we forgive those who sin against us? *'Seventy times and seven'* (v22) represents, in Jewish tradition, a number without limit.

Faith sharing

1. How difficult is it to forgive those who hurt you most?

2. How difficult is it to admit to the times when you have hurt others? Do you find it easy to apologise?

3. Is Jesus here being totally unrealistic? Is there a situation in your own life where forgiveness and reconciliation are needed? Could you take the initiative?

Faith in Action

1. What do you think you could do practically to be a force for reconciliation in your own locality or in the wider community?

2. Could you support the work of the *United Nations Association* whose members support the ideals of international reconciliation? Could you become a member?

3. Are there issues of reconciliation in your own church or between churches in your locality that you could address?

Some books for further reading

No Future Without Forgiveness by Desmond Tutu, published by Rider Books 1999, *ISBN 0-7126-7013-0*
Peacemaking for Churches by Yvonne Joan Craig, published by SPCK 1999, *ISBN 0-281-05177-1*
Reconciled Being, Love in Chaos, by Mary McAleese, published by Medio Media 1997, *ISBN 0-85305-444-4*
When the Powers Fall: Reconciliation in the Healing of the Nations, by Walter Wink, published Augsburg Fortress Publishers 1998, *ISBN 0-8006-3127-7*
On Forgiveness by Richard Holloway, published by Canongate 2002, *ISBN 1-84195-358-X*

*

Postscript

BREAKING THE BRIDGE
He that cannot forgive others
breaks the bridge over which he must pass himself;
for every man has need to be forgiven.

(Thomas Fuller)

*

BURYING THE HATCHET
There's no point in burying the hatchet
if you're going to put up a marker on the site

(Sydney Harris)

*

SEVENTY TIMES AND SEVEN
O man, forgive thy mortal foe,
nor ever strike him blow for blow;
for all the souls on earth that live,
to be forgiven must forgive;
forgive him seventy times and seven,
for all the blessed souls in heaven
are both forgivers and forgiven.

(Anon)

*

Closing worship

In your prayers remember
* the government and people of South Africa
* the work and witness of the churches of South Africa
* your own relationships especially where there has been a breach
of trust

Leader

As tools come to be sharpened by the blacksmith, so
we came, Lord. As sharpened tools go back with their
owner, so may we go back to our everyday life to be
used by thee.
Amen.

(from Africa)

Leader   The cross
All   **we shall take it**

The bread
we shall break it

The pain
we shall bear it

The joy
we shall share it

The gospel
we shall live it

The love
we shall give it

The light
we shall treasure it

The darkness
God shall perish it.

Alleluia! Amen!

6

When Bad Things Happen

'Therefore I will not restrain my mouth;
I will speak in the anguish of my spirit;
I will complain in the bitterness of my soul.'
(Job 7:11)

Theme

Sometimes bad things happen out of the blue. It may be a serious illness, an accident, a death or some other traumatic event. We ask the question 'Why?' but often find no answers or, at least, not the answers we're looking for. We ask why bad things happen to good people. We say it just isn't fair when bad people seem to go through life with apparently no burdens to carry, yet things, horrible and tragic things, happen to us and we're left angry and hurt. We need to blame somebody so we find ourselves turning to God and blaming God - but the anger is never resolved. Is there some other way we can deal with such pain and resentment?

Opening prayer

Leader

O God,
as we gather to ask deep questions
we pray for the guidance of your Spirit in all things;
when we feel helpless and life seems out of control,
grant us courage and strength that we may cope;
when we are tired and have nothing left to give,
lift our eyes and renew our hope for tomorrow;
when we are broken and feel totally alone,
touch our hearts and assure us of your continuing love;
for these are the promises of Jesus Christ your Son.
Amen.

Readings

The writer of the first extract, Rabbi Reeve Robert Brenner, is a survivor of the Nazi concentration camp at Auschwitz. The writer of the second extract is Dr Martin Luther King, the American Baptist minister and human rights activist who penned these words four years before his assassination in 1968.

I

It never occurred to me to question God's doings while I was an inmate of Auschwitz, although, of course, I understand others did... I was no less or no more religious because of what the Nazis did to us; and I believe my faith in God was not undermined in the least. It never occurred to me to associate the calamity we were experiencing with God, to blame him, or to believe in him less or cease believing in him at all because he didn't come to our aid.

God doesn't owe us that, or anything. We owe our lives to him. If someone believes God is responsible for the death of six million because he didn't somehow do something to save them, he's got his thinking reversed. We owe God our lives for the few or many years we live, and we have the duty to worship him and do as he commands us. That's what we're here on earth for, to be in God's service, to do God's bidding.

(from 'The Faith and Doubt of Holocaust Survivors'
quoted by Harold Kushner p93)

II

A positive religious faith does not offer an illusion that we shall be exempt from pain and suffering, nor does it imbue us with the idea that life is a drama of unalloyed comfort and untroubled ease. Rather, it instils us with the inner equilibrium needed to face strains, burdens, and fears that inevitably come, and assures us that the universe is trustworthy and that God is concerned.

Irreligion, on the other hand, would have us believe that we are orphans cast into the terrifying immensities of space in a universe that is without purpose or intelligence. Such a view drains courage and exhausts the energies of men.

This faith (of ours) transforms the whirlwind of despair into a warm and reviving breeze of hope. The words of a motto which a generation ago were commonly found on the wall in the homes of devout persons need to be etched on our hearts:

Fear knocked at the door.

Faith answered.

There was no one there.

(from 'Strength to Love' by Martin Luther King)

*

Sharing our own experiences

1. Share with the group a time when something bad happened to you.

2. In what way has the event or situation left its mark? Do you think you are still damaged by it?

3. Life is unfair with the wrong people getting ill and getting robbed and dying in accidents. How do *you* cope with life's unfairness?

*

Scripture reading

2 Samuel 12:15b-23

King David committed adultery with Bathsheba, the wife of one of David's most faithful soldiers, Uriah, who was later killed in battle. A baby was born but very soon the child became ill. While there was hope that his son might recover David prayed continually and he refused to eat for seven days. But then the child died. David's reaction surprised those around him. He washed himself, changed his clothes and asked for food (v20).

David had gone beyond the self-pity and self-recrimination into which he'd sunk. Either he continued to blame himself for what had happened and sink further into lethargy and depression or he got on with his life and with his responsibilities. He chose the latter. It's not an easy choice to make but perhaps for some of us it's one that we *have* to make not only for the sake of others in our lives but also for ourselves. Somehow and somewhere *there is* life beyond tragedy.

Faith sharing

1. Have you or someone close to you ever suffered deep depression? What has been the effect on your and other people's lives?

2. Have you ever blamed yourself for something bad that's happened to someone else? Does King David's experience ring bells with you?

3. Where has God been for you in times of bereavement and personal suffering?

Faith in Action

1. If you are still hurting from something bad that happened to you what new steps could you take towards dealing with it?

2. You might like to contact a centre that specialises in *Christian healing*. Your minister or local library will probably be able to suggest one near you. Alternatively you could contact a group such as the *Acorn Healing Trust* in Hampshire or *Burrswood* in Kent for further information.

3. Could you consider volunteering to work at your local hospital or hospice – perhaps in the café or shop?

Some books for further reading

When Bad Things Happen to Good People by Harold S. Kushner, published by Pan Macmillan, 2002, *ISBN 0-330-49055-9*
The Bridge of San Luis Rey by Thornton Wilder, published by Penguin 2000, *ISBN 0-14-118425-6*

Waymarks by Peter Millar, published by Canterbury Press 2000, *ISBN 1-85311-336-0*

The Faith and Doubts of Holocaust Survivors by Reeve Robert Brenner, published by Jason Aaronson Inc 1980, *ISBN 0-7657-5993-4*

Strength to Love by Martin Luther King, published by Walker & Co, US 1996, *ISBN 0-8027-2472-8*

*

Postscript

ALL SHALL BE WELL

I should have left off this worrying;
nevertheless, I mourned and sorrowed over it
without reason or discretion.
But Jesus, who in the showing told me all that I needed,
answered by this word and said:
'Sin is behovely[10] - it had to be - but all shall be well,
and all shall be well,
and all manner of thing shall be well.'
(Julian of Norwich, born c1342 and died after 1413)

*

BLAMING GOD

When the Russian poet Yevgeny Yevtuschenko was able to visit the West he imagined that everyone he would meet would be a Christian. He heard that the English novelist Kingsley Amis was an atheist so when he met him he said: 'You don't believe in God, do you?'

'No,' Amis replied. 'Well, actually, it's more that I hate the bastard.'

*

SELF-LOATHING

My own heart let me have more have pity on; let
Me live to my sad self hereafter kind,
Charitable; not live this tormented mind
With this tormented mind tormenting yet.
I cast for comfort I can no more get
By groping round my comfortless, than blind
Eyes in their dark can day or thirst can find
Thirst's all-in-all in all a world of wet.

(from 'Poems 1918' by Gerard Manley Hopkins, 1844–89)

Closing worship

In your prayers remember

* those who suffer from trauma and tragedy

*those who minister to them in hospitals, churches and advice centres

* your own healing of past hurts and painful memories

Leader

> Grant your healing, O God, to those who suffer in body, mind or spirit;
> grant your peace, O Christ, to those who can only watch and wait;
> grant your strength, O Spirit, to those who need to be carried;
> and grant your blessing, Father, Son and Holy Spirit, to your servants gathered here.
> **Amen.**

Leader I lie down with God
All   may God lie down with me
        I sleep with God
        may God be present in my dreams
        I trust in God
        may God protect me from all danger
        I rise with God
        may God rise with me
        I walk with God
        may God be always at my side
        I rely on God
        may God strengthen me in my labour
        I eat with God
        may God be in my bread
        I drink with God
        may God be in my wine
        I live with God
        may God live within me.
        Amen.

(a Celtic prayer)

7

The Good Earth

'God saw everything that he had made, and indeed,
it was very good.'
(Genesis 1:31)

Theme

We all live on the good earth but much of it is being polluted. Many species of plant and animal life are facing extinction, greenhouse gases are changing the climate, low-lying countries face increased flooding as ice-bergs and glaciers melt and our very health is being threatened by the air we breathe.

Developing countries are industrialising in order to create the jobs their peoples need but the pollution that results is only adding to the problems already caused by industry in the United States and Europe.

How, then, do we express our concerns for the future of our planet so that we hand on to our children and our children's children a home that is fit to live in but without advocating policies that will only cause more hunger and suffering in the poorest countries of the world?

Opening prayer

Leader

Almighty God, we come together to thank you for
the beauty and glory of your creation; to praise you
for your holiness and grace; to acknowledge our
responsibility to the animal kingdom and for our use of
the created world.

All	Creator God, you have given us temporary lordship of your beautiful creation. But we have misused our power, turned away from responsibility and marred your image in us. Forgive us, true Lord, and help us to follow the way of your Son, Jesus Christ, who expressed power in humility and lordship in loving service. Enable us, by your Spirit, to walk in newness of life, healing injury, avoiding wrong and making peace with all your creatures. Amen.

(from the RSPCA Order of Service for Animal Welfare)

Reading

This is the text of a BBC Radio 4 'Thought for the Day' given by the Rt Revd Bill Westwood when he was Bishop of Peterborough.

The remorseless logic of nature - that if one thing happens another will follow! Last hot summer I didn't water the newly planted trees enough. They died. Nobody said "that was unlucky, try harder next year." The trees just died. Scientists spend their lives grappling with this logic but it's not easy.

I tried to follow the programme about Einstein in Science Week, but when I got to the bit about space being curved, I gave up. But believing, as I do, in a God of creation and order, I have a respect for those who try to struggle with what order in Nature can mean.

At the beginning of the Bible there's a similar struggle. Here are two stories of Creation one of which is of a Creation with Man at the centre, with orders to have dominion, subdue and rule the world. The other, older by about 400 years, is about Man set in the Garden, to tend and care for it.

Both are great myths, written by ancient people as they struggle to find meaning, but ancient as they are, they still carry force. For generations we have seen Man the Ruler, dominating the natural world, using the forests and fields, the seas and animal kingdom, for his own purpose and pleasure. It seems it's only recently that we've begun to hear the message of the other story, that Man, a part of Creation, not different from it, for it belongs to God, has to care for and guard the forests and the fields, the seas and the animals.

Our present anxieties about BSE, the cries of the thoughtful ecologist, the concerns about thoughtless cruelty towards animals, are perhaps signs that we are moving towards re-thinking our relationship with Nature, for we are coming to realise that we are not Kings of the Universe, but we are more like Gardeners: clever, experienced knowledgeable, but gardeners all the same. It's a much more humble stance, of course, and one we might not be keen to follow, but if we don't, then the remorseless logic of Nature could drive us there.

(Rt Revd Bill Westwood, 1996)

Sharing our own experiences

1. Share some of your own concerns about creation.

2. What do you think are the most critical environmental issues facing the planet in the next few years?

3. What limits do you think there are to taking direct action (e.g. what laws can be justifiably broken, if any) in protecting the environment? Do you think violence is ever justified in pursuit of any such aim? Does the end justify the means?

Scripture reading

The first Creation story concluding with the creation of Humankind: Genesis 1:26-2:3

The second Creation story with Adam and Eve in the Garden: Genesis 2:4b-25

The purpose of these two Genesis stories is not to explain the mechanics of creation but to answer the question 'Why does everything exist?' Christians believe that Creation exists because there is a Creator behind it all. This Prime Cause – whom we call God - gives the Creation the purpose and meaning most people have struggled to find throughout human history.

The Genesis stories lay a responsibility upon all of humankind to care for creation because it belongs not to us but to God. We are stewards answerable to him. However, if there were no personal creator then some might say that it's much harder to argue that we have a moral responsibility towards creation than is *universally* acceptable. Even so it's the industrialised Christian countries that have caused much of the damage so how seriously do we take the teachings of Genesis?

Faith sharing

1. Do you ever feel close to the creation? If so, when and why?

2. How can we balance our need for economic progress with the need to preserve the environment given that we in the West are already rich compared to the majority of people on earth?

3. Do you see a conflict between the two creation stories? Why do you think in recent years the injunction to subdue the earth has taken priority over the command to tend the garden and care for it?

Faith in Action

1. Write to the *RSPCA, Greenpeace* or *Friends of the Earth* for further information. Maybe join a local group.

2. Contact *Animal Christian Concern, A Rocha* or *Christian Ecology Link* for further information. Perhaps have a *Pets Service* or *Environment Service* in your church.

3. Explore what environmental issues there may be in your locality and perhaps get involved!

4. Support *Christian Aid* in their campaigns on behalf of the world's poor. Consider joining their email campaign network.

Some books for further reading

The Good Earth by Pearl Buck, published Simon and Schuster 1999, *ISBN 0-671-03577-0*

Rich Christians in an Age of Hunger by Ronald J. Sider, published 1978, *ISBN: 0-340-22810-5*

God is Green: Ecology for Christians, by Ian C. Bradley, published 1992 *ISBN: 0-385-42279-2*

Small is Beautiful: Economics as if People Mattered by E. F. Schumacher, published 1973 *ISBN: 0-09-922561-1*

*

Postscript

WHAT IS A CHARITABLE HEART?
What is a charitable heart?
It is a heart which is burning with love
for the whole creation -
a heart which is softened
and can no longer bear to see or learn from others
of any suffering,
even the smallest pain,
being inflicted upon a creature
(St Isaac the Syrian c347-438)
*

A ROBIN
A robin redbreast in a cage
puts all heaven in a rage
(William Blake 1757-1827)
*

WHY DOES MAN DESTROY?
The sun rose from behind the mountain,
crowning the tops of trees with diadems of gold.
I asked myself,
'Why does Man destroy that which nature builds?'
(from 'A Lamentation in the Field'
by Khalil Gibran 1883-1931)

*

Closing worship

In your prayers remember
* the good earth that God has given to us and the many blessings we receive from it
* humankind's responsibility to steward the earth wisely
* organisations and pressure groups who work on behalf of the good earth

Leader

> May the raindrops fall lightly on your brow
> May the soft winds freshen your spirit
> May the sunshine brighten your heart
> May the burdens of the day rest lightly upon you
> And may God enfold you in the mantle of his love.
> **Amen.**
>
> *(a Celtic prayer)*

Leader   Creator God, bless us this night
All   **and bless your creation**

Creator God, grant us peace this night
and grant us a share in your redemption

Creator God, renew us by your Holy Spirit
and help us to care for all you have made

Father, Son and Holy Spirit
help us to praise you for all your marvellous works.

Amen.

8

Direct Action

'But someone will say, 'You have faith and I have works.'
Show me your faith without works, and I by my works
will show you my faith.'
(James 2:18)

Theme

Sometimes praying, signing petitions and writing letters isn't
enough when we feel strongly about an issue. We want to do
something more. We might go on a protest march or take part in a
vigil or demonstration. For some Christians, though, breaking one law
in order to keep a higher law is the chosen path. For them arrest, a fine
or even a term in prison is the price they are prepared to pay in support
of their deeply held beliefs.

Opening prayer

Leader

> We are here, God.
> We have felt your touch in the sunlight
> and seen your power in the salt waves.
> We have wondered at your mystery in the stars
> and we marvel that the maker of the universe
> knows us by name.

All

> **We are here God.**
> **We have come to hear your voice speaking to**
> **us.**

We are here, Jesus.
We know that you came to find us.
We have listened to your words
and smiled at your stories.

We have felt the warmth of your love
and we thank you that you have called us friends.

We are here, Jesus.
We have come to hear your voice speaking to
us.

We are here, Holy Spirit.
We are grateful for your presence,
grateful for the way you bring us close -
for the way you comfort and challenge us
and keep us right.

We are here, Holy Spirit.
We have come to hear your voice speaking to
us.

(from 'The Pattern of our Days' edited by Kathy Galloway, adapted)

Reading

In 1999 Ellen Moxley, a Quaker and a member of the Iona Community, was one of three women (together with Angie Zelter and Ulla Roder) who peacefully entered the 'Maytime', an acoustic testing platform in Loch Goil in Scotland. It was closely connected with the operation of British Trident nuclear submarines so they cleared out its laboratory, throwing computers and other equipment into the deep waters of the loch. They then sat down to have a picnic and watch the sunset. The three were arrested and charged with causing malicious damage to a Trident-related system.

Ellen's argument was that because the use of nuclear weapons had been declared unlawful in an historic judgement by the International Court of Justice in 1996 she was helping *prevent* their potential use and, therefore, she was *preventing* a potential crime being committed by the UK government. Her argument was that any government threatening to use Trident would be engaged in a criminal conspiracy to carry out crimes against humanity and that would be against established international humanitarian law.[11] Ellen and her two co-defendants were found not guilty and were discharged.

A number of countries presently have a nuclear capability including the USA, Russia, China, France, India, Pakistan and the UK and perhaps others. In the UK there is only one way of delivering a nuclear warhead and that is by Trident (the Polaris and Vulcan nuclear bomber systems are both now obsolete).

The UK has four Trident nuclear-powered submarines although normally only one submarine is deployed at sea with its missiles at any one time. Since 1998, that one submarine carries 16 missiles with three warheads of 100 kilotons each - eight times more powerful than the Hiroshima bomb. The whole Trident fleet has a combined destructive power of 1200 Hiroshimas. However, the missiles have been de-targeted and are now on several days notice' to fire.

The Just War rules, the Geneva Conventions and subsequent legislation based on them protect non-combatants in time of war. The deliberate killing of civilians has always been regarded as a war crime - such as the extermination of six million Jews in the Holocaust and the atrocities we have seen in more recent years in former Yugoslavia, Rwanda and East Timor.

Nuclear bombs are indiscriminate in their effects. Not only would military and civilian personnel be killed or maimed but the land would be polluted for years to come (affecting future generations of children yet unborn and therefore not party to the conflict) and the atmosphere would carry the radiation hazard beyond international boundaries (as happened after the Chernobyl incident) so polluting land and injuring people in countries also not party to the conflict.

Apart from the humanitarian consequences the litigation

demanding compensation that could follow would be enormous in its economic effects. The clean-up costs after the use of nuclear weapons would be prohibitive for generations to come. It was to prevent this scenario that Ellen and her two friends engaged in their non-violent preventative action.

At their trial they called a number of expert witnesses while the UK government offered no evidence to the contrary. In acquitting the women the Sheriff found there was no criminal intent because their actions were based on a sincere belief that they were acting to prevent the UK government contravening international humanitarian law. The jury were instructed by the Sheriff to return *Not Guilty* verdicts. However, the legal issues Ellen and her two friends raised were subsequently referred to higher courts which have since rejected their defence.

(Ellen Moxley's story told with permission)

Sharing our own experiences

1. What do you think about Ellen Moxley's decision to take part in non-violent direct action?

2. Nuclear weapons have been declared unlawful by the International Court of Justice on the basis that their use would necessarily cause the deaths of non-combatants and so constitute a war crime. What do you feel about this?

3. The International Court of Justice argues that people are *citizens with rights* rather than *state property* to be used. In a world of increasing globalisation what do you feel about this?

Scripture reading

Matthew 5:1-12

In the Beatitudes we are reminded of the ideals to which all Christians should aspire including that of peace*making* (which may not be the same, of course, as just being peace*able*). You might think of examples. Each Beatitude brings a promise of blessing and that takes us to the heart of Christ's teaching - that God is himself the prime source of blessing to all those who will respond to him. The Ten Beatitudes given by Jesus on the Mount are both personal and social in their application in the same way as the Ten Commandments were when they were given by Moses on Mount Sinai over a thousand years before.

Faith sharing

1. What do the Beatitudes mean for you? Which ones speak to you most?

2. What does it mean to be a peacemaker? Can peacemaking ever include violence either of word or action?

3. Do you think there is a difference between the use of force and the use of violence?

4. Globalisation, capitalism and animal welfare concerns are examples of other issues that have generated major protests and direct action around the world. Do you think the protestors' concerns are justified?

*

Faith in Action

1. You might like to find our more about *CND* or *Christian CND*.

2. You might like to contact the *Quakers (the Religious Society of Friends)* who are pacifists and whose members have been conscientious objectors in times of war.

3. Contact the *Iona Community* or the *Scottish Centre for Non-Violence* for further information on issues of justice and peace.

4. Contact the *World Court Project* website *www.gn.apc.org/wcp* for fuller information on the legal issues raised by Ellen Moxley's action.

*

Some books for further reading

Engaging the Powers by Walter Wink, published 1959,
ISBN 0-8006-2646-X
The Powers that Be by Walter Wink, published 1999
ISBN 0-385-48752-5
Christianity & War in a Nuclear Age by Richard Harries, published by
Mowbray 1986, *ISBN 0-264-67053-1*

*

Postscript

WHERE IS THEIR HOMELAND?

Then I looked toward the city of the living
and said in my soul,
'That is for the rich and the powerful.'
Then I looked toward the city of the dead and said,
'This, too, is for the rich and the powerful.
O Lord,
where is the homeland for the poor and weak?'
(from 'In the City of the Dead' by Khalil Gibran 1883-1931)

*

THIS FRAGILE, DELICATE EARTH

'It's a question of our relationship with
each other and with this fragile, delicate earth.'
(Ellen Moxley concluding her testimony)

*

THE GOOD EARTH

Bless to us, O God,
The morning sun that is above us,
The good earth that is beneath us,
The friends that are around us,
Your image deep within us,
The day that is before us.
(from the Celtic tradition)

*

CHRIST HAS NO HANDS BUT OUR HANDS

Christ has no hands but our hands
To do His work today,
He has no feet but our feet
To lead men in His way;
He has no tongues but our tongues
To tell men how He died,
He has no help but our help
To bring men to His side.

We are the only Bible
The careless world will read,
We are the sinner's gospel
We are the scoffer's creed;
We are the Lord's last message
Given in deed and word,
What if the type is crooked?
What if the print is blurred?
What if our hands are busy
With other things than His?
What if our feet are walking
Where sin's allurement is?
What if our tongues are speaking
Of things His life would spurn,
How can we hope to help Him
And welcome His return?

(Annie J. Flint 1934)

Closing worship

In your prayers remember
* those whose commitment leads them to take direct action
* the consequences of direct action for families and friends
* the situations that are the cause of people taking direct action

Leader

Creator God, we bless you for our homes and loved
ones:
for those who love us even when we are hard to love
and for those who need our love each and every day

Jesus Christ, we bless you because you love us:
you have called us your friends
and you promise to be our companion on the way
Holy Spirit, we bless you because you are the bringer
of life:
you are the unpredictable breath of God
and you lead us to where we should be.

All

Creator God, redeeming Son
and liberating Spirit
you have called us to tread dangerous paths
and travel exciting ways;
bless us as we journey from this place
that we may be a blessing
to all those we meet on the way.
Amen.

(from the Celtic tradition)

Leader	On our hearts and our houses
All	**The blessing of God**

In our coming and going
The peace of God

In our life and believing
The love of God

At our end and new beginning
**The arms of God to welcome us
and bring us home.
Amen.**

*(from 'The Pattern of Our Days'
edited by Kathy Galloway)*

9

Welcoming the Stranger?

'You shall not oppress a resident alien;
you know the heart of an alien for you were aliens in the land of Egypt.'
(Exodus 23:9)

Theme

The arrival in Britain of asylum seekers and economic migrants has become a major issue since the fall of communism in 1989 and raises a number of moral as well as practical issues. How should Christians respond to the needs of the stranger but how should we also respond to the concerns of those communities most affected by them? And how, indeed, do we combat the prejudices and half-truths that cloud any mature discussion of the issue?

Opening prayer

Leader

Lord God: some of us are like the Shepherds –
just carrying out our jobs
despite the turbulence of the world around us.
Give us a message…. send us an angel
to help us seek a new way of living.

All

Lord God: others of us are like the Wise Men
from the East –
we see the need of some power
to come and give us direction
but we don't know in which direction to go.

**Give us the wisdom to see
that it is not in physical power that our
salvation lies
but in love and humility.**

Leader

Lord God: a few of us are like Herod —
we don't want a new power to enter the world
in case it might threaten our own power.
Give us the humility to be ready
for new ways of doing things.

All

**Lord God:
we ask you to make us expectant
instead of planners;
to make us seekers
rather than know-alls.
We ask you for grace
so that we are ready to receive from you
and from one another.
Amen.**
(George MacLeod, adapted)

*

Reading

Bryan Owen has been involved with the Balkans since 1991. For several years he helped organise the re-training of Albanian doctors in Scottish hospitals. In 1997 he represented the British Churches at the Albanian elections and later helped supervise the UN-sponsored elections in Kosovo in 2000. Subsequently, he has also represented the British government as an international observer at elections in FYR Macedonia and Serbia.

There are significant *migrations* of people going on in the world today. They are 'significant' because those who arrive in a country such as the UK often generate hostility on the part of the host community. When migrants come into the UK, for example, a great number of wrong assumptions are made – such as 'they' are taking money, goods and services that would otherwise have been used for the indigenous community. Immigrants are also frequently blamed for an increase in crime, accusations that are not based on facts and figures but rather more on anecdote and fear of the unknown. Immigrants, therefore, generate political tensions which Western governments are finding increasingly difficult to manage simply because of stereotyping, ignorance and downright dishonest reporting in the tabloid media.

The movement of people from the Balkans, China, Africa and the Middle East is caused by a number of often inter-connected factors. These people may be escaping from conflict (as has happened in Kosovo, Congo or Afghanistan). They may be escaping from an authoritarian regime where their lives are in danger (as happened in Iraq under Saddam Hussein or Zimbabwe under Robert Mugabe). Or they may simply be looking for a new life with job prospects and the chance of remitting money back home to their families (as has happened with migrants from China, India or Albania).

Under international law *economic migrants* are those who are escaping from poverty. They are looking for jobs. Some will be relatively unskilled compared to the host community and what skills they do have will not necessarily match the vacancies that exist at any particular time in the job market. Others such as doctors or teachers may be very skilled but for one reason or another they are not allowed to exercise those skills. The consequence may be that some migrants will find themselves working in the black economy, the sex trade, turning to crime or just living on the streets.

In 2003 the British government extended the number of categories under which it would grant *work permits*.[12] That, unfortunately, has created new ethical dilemmas. For example, in attracting nurses from countries such as the Philippines to fill the increasing number of vacancies in the UK's National Health Service the Philippines Health

Service is being denuded of qualified people it can't afford to lose. As the UK's health service is strengthened so a developing country's health service is pushed to the point of collapse. From the Filipino nurses' point of view, though, they and their families need the money they can earn in the West in order to get themselves out of poverty. Of course, there will always be more people trying to escape hunger and poverty than there are work permits available.

The other category of migrant today is the *asylum seeker*. Claiming asylum is regulated by the UN Convention on the Status of Refugees, the European Convention on Human Rights and in appropriate circumstances the UN Convention on the Rights of the Child.[13] *'Asylum'* comes from the Greek word ἀσύλου *(asulon)* meaning 'refuge'. Asylum seekers, therefore, are people seeking refuge from specific kinds of danger to their lives or the lives of their families.

Because of the restrictions on entry into the UK and elsewhere in the European Union there is a market in *people smuggling*. In 2001, for example, the going rate was around US$2,000 per person for the journey from Albania to the UK via Italy. Asylum seekers or economic migrants from the Middle East and Asia make their way to the Adriatic ports of Vlorë and Durrës in Albania where they transfer to a high speed boat for the two-hour dash to the Italian coast. Once there, lorries are waiting for the onward journey to Germany, France or the UK.

People trafficking is the smuggling of people for sexual exploitation. Often the lure for girls and young women is of good jobs in the European Union. It has been estimated that there are 30,000 Albanian prostitutes working mainly in Italy (15,000) but also in Greece (6,000) as well as in other European countries.[14] One campaigning organisation in Britain[15] says that there are 5,000 women working in the London sex trade of whom 4,000 come from Eastern Europe. Half of these were estimated to be under 18 years of age.

The international charity Save the Children reports that most prostitutes from the Balkans are subject to 'extreme levels of danger, violence and sexual exploitation'.[16] Murder by their pimps is not uncommon. For those who do manage to return home there is very little help so the problem will remain for as long as present economic conditions prevail and financial rewards for the traffickers are so high. Save the Children noted that 60 percent of Albanian trafficking victims were minors.

Scotland's *Sunday Herald* newspaper has reported that the Bosnian town of Brcko flaunts Europe's only open-air female slave market.[17] Women and girls are bought and sold, they allege, by Albanian, Romanian and Ukrainian criminal gangs for work in brothels and massage parlours throughout the European Union. The going rate for girls as young as 13 or 14 is around £2,000 each. Some were lured with promises of well-paid jobs abroad, some were coerced by parents with too many mouths to feed while others were simply kidnapped or lured into sham marriages. Save the Children claim that there is a decrease in the number of girls attending high school in Albania because of the fear of abduction especially in the northern rural areas where the traffickers mainly operate.

As well as immigration, of course, there is *emigration.* That is rarely reported by the press, however. According to the National Coalition of Anti-Deportation Campaigns more than 2 million people *left the UK for good* between 1991 and 2000. These were people who had the right of residency and the great majority were British nationals. During the period 1991 to 2000, on average some 222,800 persons emigrated from the UK each year, whilst on average around 280,100 migrated to the UK.[18] The net difference in a country of 60 million is very small indeed and decreasing.

(Bryan Owen)

*

Sharing our own experiences

1. Have you ever endured poverty? Have you ever felt totally powerless to help yourself?

2. Do you know any asylum seekers or economic migrants? Have you ever heard their stories at first hand?

3. The gospel imperative is for us to respond to human need whatever it might be. How should that best happen?

Scripture reading

Isaiah 61:1-4

These verses are full of promise for people in trouble. They were so important that Jesus used them as the basis for his first sermon in Nazareth (cf Luke 4:16-30). God anoints all of us to bring *'good news'* to people today – good news which is both practical as well as spiritual so that even *'ruined cities'* (v4) shall be repaired. How do we relate these promises to the problems of countries where there is war or a lack of personal security?

Faith sharing

1. What is the heart of Christ's 'good news' for you?

2. If his good news is for everyone does that include those who don't call themselves Christians? Does this mean that Hindus, Muslims, Buddhists and Sikhs all have to become Christians before they can be helped?

3. Does Christ's good news refer only to our personal salvation or does it extend beyond that? If so, in what way?

Faith in Action

1. Could you consider setting up a local group (perhaps including different faith communities) to study the impact of economic migrants or asylum seekers on a community near you?

2. Could you invite a speaker who works with asylum seekers to address your church or group?

3. You might like to contact the *Refugee Council* (or the *Scottish Refugee Council*) for further information.

4. Write to your *MP* or to the *Home Secretary* expressing your concerns about the UK's policy towards those generally classed as 'asylum seekers'.

*

Some books for further reading

Strange Places, Questionable People by John Simpson, published by Pan Books 1998 *ISBN 0-330-35566-X*

Saddam's Bombmaker by Khidhir Hamza, published by Touchstone 2000 *ISBN 0-684-87386-9*

My name came up – Kosovo – war, exile and return, published by the Refugee Council 2000, *ISBN 0-946787-38-7*

The Pyramid by Ismail Kadare, published by Harvill Press 1992, *ISBN 1-86046-124-7*

*

Postscript

OUR SOLEMN DUTY

'Wherever men and women
are condemned to live in extreme poverty,
human rights are violated.
To come together
to ensure that these rights be respected
is our solemn duty.'

(Joseph Wresinski, 17 October 1987
Words engraved on the Commemorative Stone at the Plaza of Liberties
and Human Rights at the Trocadero in Paris,
where in 1948 the Universal Declaration
of Human Rights was signed.)

*

THE RUNE OF HOSPITALITY

We saw a stranger yesterday,
We put food in the eating place,
Drink in the drinking place,
Music in the listening place,
And, with the sacred name of the Triune God,
He blessed us and our house,
Our cattle and our dear ones.
As the lark says in her song:
Often, often, often,
Goes Christ in the stranger's guise.
(traditional Celtic)

*

WELCOME THE STRANGER

All guests who present themselves are to be welcomed as Christ, for
he himself will say: 'I was a stranger and you welcomed me'
(Matthew 25:35).

(Rule of St Benedict, Chapter 53)

*

Closing worship

In your prayers remember
    * all refugees wherever they are
    * those who work in refugee camps on our behalf
    * the United Nations High Commission for Refugees

Leader

Teach us, good Lord, to serve thee as thou deservest,
to give and not to count the cost, to fight and not
to heed the wounds, to toil and not to seek for rest,
to labour and not to ask for any reward, save that of
knowing that we do thy will; through Jesus Christ our
Lord.
Amen.

(prayer of St Ignatius Loyola)

All

**Be present, O merciful God, and protect us
through the silent hours of this night, so
that we who are wearied by the changes and
chances of this fleeting world, may repose
upon thy eternal changelessness; through
Jesus Christ our Lord.
Amen.**

(from the Leonine Sacramentary)

10

Fear of the Future

'Do not boast about tomorrow,
for you do not know what a day may bring.'
(Proverbs 27:1)

Theme

For many of us the future is exciting and full of promise and possibilities. For others, though, the future is something we fear or even dread because it brings with it uncertainty and threat. Many of us 'live for today for tomorrow we die' – and that is one *certainty* in the future most of us try not to think about. But the essence of the Christian life is the possibility for change and growth – and even our own death is part of that wider vision of redemption. Our Christian belief is that death is not the end for in Christ death itself has been overcome.

Opening prayer

Leader

Gracious and Holy Father,
give us wisdom to perceive you,
diligence to seek you,
patience to wait for you,
eyes to behold you,
a heart to meditate on you,
and a life to proclaim you,
through the power of the Spirit
of Jesus Christ our Lord.
Amen.

(a prayer of St Benedict)

Reading

Richard's girlfriend, Karen, has been in a coma for seventeen years but he's faithfully waited for her all that time. Suddenly she wakes up. Richard and his friends have to learn new ways of being truly themselves. In this extract Karen is speaking to Richard and their friends about the future.

"Plan B is this. You're to be different now. Your behaviour will be changing. Your thinking is to change. And people will watch these changes in you and they'll come to experience the world in your new manner."

"*How*?" Richard asks. "How do we change?"

"Richard, tell me this: back in the old world, didn't you often feel as if the only way you could fully *truly* change yourself in the powerful way you yearned for was to die and start then again from scratch? Didn't you feel as if all the symbols and ideas fed to you since birth had become worn out like old shoes? Didn't you ache for change but you didn't know how to achieve it? And even if you knew how to do it, would you have had the guts to go forth? Didn't you want your cards shuffled in a different way?"

"Yeah. Sure. But didn't everybody?"

"No. Not always. This feeling is so specific to the times we live in."

"Okay..."

"And Richard, haven't you always felt that you live forever on the brink of knowing a great truth? Well, that feeling is true. There *is* the truth. It does exist."

"A*ha*!"

"Yes. Well, now it's going to be as if you've died and were reincarnated but you stay inside your own body. For all of you. And in your new lives you'll have to live entirely for that one sensation – that of imminent truth. And you're going to have to holler for it, steal for it, beg for it – and you're never going to stop asking questions about it twenty-four hours a day, for the rest of your life.

"This is Plan B.

"Every day for the rest of your lives, all of your living moments are to be spent making others aware of this need – the need to probe and drill and examine and locate the words that take us to beyond ourselves.

"Scrape. Feel. Dig. Believe. *Ask.*

"Ask questions, no, *screech* questions out loud – while kneeling in front of the electric doors at Safeway..."

"What do we ask?" Wendy asks.

"Ask whatever challenges dead and thoughtless beliefs. Ask: *When did we become human beings and stop being whatever we were before this? Ask: What was the specific change that made us human? Ask: Why do people not particularly care about their ancestors more than three generations back? Ask: Why are we unable to think of any real future beyond, say, a hundred years from now? Ask: How can we begin to think of the future as something enormous before us that also includes us? Ask: Having become human, what is it that we are now doing or creating that will transform us into whatever it is that we are slated to next become?"*

(from 'Girlfriend in a Coma' by Douglas Coupland, pp 268-271)

*

Sharing our own experiences

1. Do you feel as if all *'the symbols and ideas fed to you since birth'* need changing? Do you fear the loss of old absolutes?

2. What *'dead and thoughtless'* beliefs would you like to challenge?

3. Do you think the world will be a better or worse place in the future? Why?

Scripture reading

2 Corinthians 5:16-21

St Paul assures us that when we become a Christian we become a *'new creation'* (v17). The old has passed away and the new has come. Of course, we are still the same person with the same faults we had before. But now we have new motivation and new priorities – we want to live for God rather than for ourselves. Through faith in Christ we are reconciled to God and are safe in his hands. Because of this change in our outlook on life we in our turn can become *'ambassadors for Christ'* (v20) so that through us he can reach out to others. Do you consider yourself to be such an ambassador?

*

Faith sharing

1. When did you become a believing Christian – was it through a sudden conversion experience or was it more gradual?

2. Do you feel that your faith helps you to see yourself as a new person in Christ where *'the old has gone and, behold, the new has come'?*

3. Do you believe in life after death – or merely hope for it?

*

Faith in Action

1. Could you commit yourself to making the future for someone somewhere more hopeful than it otherwise might be?

2. Have you thought about joining a *political party* through which you could work for a better future for us all?

3. Having reached the end of this course is there *an issue* that you have previously studied that you could now commit yourself to?

*

Some books for further reading

Girlfriend in a Coma by Douglas Coupland, published by Flamingo 1998, *ISBN 0-00-655127-0*

Toward the End of Time by John Updike, published by Penguin 1999, *ISBN 0-14-027143-0*

Brave New World by Aldous Huxley, published by Flamingo 1994, *ISBN 0-00-654579-3*

Against Love by Laura Kipnis, published by Pantheon Books 2003, *ISBN 0-375-42189-0*

Six Questions That Can Change Your Life, by Joseph Nowinski, published by Rodale Ltd 2002 *ISBN 1-405-02097-0*

*

Postscript

THE FUTURE
I never think of the future.
It comes soon enough.
(Albert Einstein)

*

THE FUTURE
The best thing about the future is that
it comes only one day at a time.
(Abraham Lincoln)

*

TIME
Time is a three-fold present:
the present as we experience it,
the past as a present memory,
and the future as a present expectation.
(St Augustine of Hippo)

*

THIS LIFE

This life is not a state of being righteous,
but, rather, of growth in righteousness;
not a state of being healthy,
but a period of healing;
not a state of being,
but becoming;
not a state of rest,
but of exercise and activity.
We are not yet what we shall be,
but we grow towards it;

the process is not yet finished,
but is still going on;
this life is not the end,
it is the way to a better.
All does not yet shine with glory;
nevertheless, all is being purified.[19]

(Martin Luther 1483-1546)

Closing worship

In your prayers remember
* those who are afraid of the future
* politicians who plan for the future
* that you might live in the power of the resurrection

Leader

>We cannot pray to you, O God, to end war –
>for we know that you have made the world in such a way
>that we must find our own path to peace
>within ourselves and with our neighbours

All

>**We cannot pray to you, O God, to end starvation –
>for you have already given us the resources
>with which to feed the entire world
>if only we would use them wisely**

>We cannot pray to you, O God, to root out prejudice –
>for you have already given us eyes
>with which to see the good in everyone
>if only we would use them rightly

>**We cannot pray to you, O God, to end despair –
>for you have already given us the power
>to clear away slums and to give hope
>if only we would use our power justly**

>We cannot pray to you, O God, to end disease –
>for you have already given us great minds with which
>to search out cures and healing
>if only we would use them constructively

>**Therefore we pray to you instead, O God
>for strength, determination and willpower**

to do instead of just pray
to become instead of merely to wish.
 Amen.

(from 'Likrat Shabbat',
prayer by Rabbi Jack Riemer)

All   O God, in your mercy
forgive what we have been,
sanctify what we are
and order what we shall be.
What we know not, teach us,
what we have not, give us,
and what we are not, make us,
so that we may travel into the future
knowing that you are with us always. Amen.

(source unknown)

As you GO into

GOD'S WORLD -

May the RAINDROPS fall lightly on

YOUR BROW,

May the SOFT WINDS freshen

YOUR SPIRIT,

May the SUNSHINE brighten

YOUR HEART,

May the BURDENS OF THE DAY rest lightly

UPON YOU,

And may GOD enfold you in the mantle of

HIS LOVE.

(a Celtic blessing)

References

[1] I John 4:20-21

[2] James 2:14-17

[3] John 10:10

[4] cf *Status Anxiety* by Alain de Botton, pp 67-91, published 2004 by Hamish Hamilton, ISBN 0-241-14238-5

[5] Dr Runcie was quoting from the 19th century Chicago journalist Finley Peter Dunne who wrote, *"The newspaper does everything for us. It runs the police force and the banks, commands the militia, controls the legislature, baptises the young, marries the foolish, comforts the afflicted, afflicts the comfortable, buries the dead and roasts them afterward."*
This has become a basic tenet of journalism.

[6] Matthew 27:46

[7] Names, addresses, telephone numbers and websites are all listed in Appendix III, page 127

[8] *Daw* is the respectful salutation for a widow, *Aung San* is her father's name, and *Suu Kyi* is her own name. Today she is often referred to as *Daw Suu*.

[9] The military regime has renamed Burma *Myanmar* and Rangoon *Yangon*. These changes are not recognised by the opposition.

[10] to be necessary

[11] The Geneva Conventions generally protect non-combatants such as children, women, the sick and the elderly; a nuclear bomb would indiscriminately kill combatants and non-combatants alike.

[12] cf The Immigration, Nationality and Asylum Act 2002

[13] cf Appendix II, page 123, for details

[14] From a report by Daniel Renton of Save the Children 2001 quoted in BESA magazine Vol 5 2002

[15] *'End Child Prostitution, Pornography and Trafficking'* (quoted in 'The Observer' early in 2003)

[16] cf *Tricked into Prostitution* 2002 and *State of the World's Mothers* 2002

[17] *'The Sunday Herald'*, 7 April 2002

[18] Statistics taken from the Annual Abstract of Statistics

[19] 2 Corinthians 3:18

[20] UN Convention on the Status of Refugees 1.A.2

[21] The Foreign Office Country Report, the US State Department Country Report, and reports from Amnesty International and Human Rights Watch are the ones usually made available

[22] *'Secure Borders, Safe Haven'*, HMSO 2001, 4.9 and 4.14

[23] op cit 4.12

[24] sources: *Department of Work and Pensions* and *The Observer* on 23 May 2004

Appendix 1
The UN Declaration of Human Rights

Article 1.

All human beings are born free and equal in dignity and rights. They are endowed with reason and conscience and should act towards one another in a spirit of brotherhood.

Article 2.

Everyone is entitled to all the rights and freedoms set forth in this Declaration, without distinction of any kind, such as race, colour, sex, language, religion, political or other opinion, national or social origin, property, birth or other status. Furthermore, no distinction shall be made on the basis of the political, jurisdictional or international status of the country or territory to which a person belongs, whether it be independent, trust, non-self-governing or under any other limitation of sovereignty.

Article 3.

Everyone has the right to life, liberty and security of person.

Article 4.

No one shall be held in slavery or servitude; slavery and the slave trade shall be prohibited in all their forms.

Article 5.

No one shall be subjected to torture or to cruel, inhuman or degrading treatment or punishment.

Article 6.

Everyone has the right to recognition everywhere as a person before the law.

Article 7.

All are equal before the law and are entitled without any discrimination to equal protection of the law. All are entitled to equal protection against any discrimination in violation of this Declaration and against any incitement to such discrimination.

Article 8.

Everyone has the right to an effective remedy by the competent national tribunals for acts violating the fundamental rights granted him by the constitution or by law.

Article 9.

No one shall be subjected to arbitrary arrest, detention or exile.

Article 10.

Everyone is entitled in full equality to a fair and public hearing by an independent and impartial tribunal, in the determination of his rights and obligations and of any criminal charge against him.

Article 11.

(1) Everyone charged with a penal offence has the right to be presumed innocent until proved guilty according to law in a public trial at which he has had all the guarantees necessary for his defence.

(2) No one shall be held guilty of any penal offence on account of any act or omission which did not constitute a penal offence, under national or international law, at the time when it was committed. Nor shall a heavier penalty be imposed than the one that was applicable at the time the penal offence was committed.

Article 12.

No one shall be subjected to arbitrary interference with his privacy, family, home or correspondence, nor to attacks upon his honour and reputation. Everyone has the right to the protection of the law against such interference or attacks.

Article 13.

(1) Everyone has the right to freedom of movement and residence within the borders of each state.

(2) Everyone has the right to leave any country, including his own, and to return to his country.

Article 14.

(1) Everyone has the right to seek and to enjoy in other countries asylum from persecution.

(2) This right may not be invoked in the case of prosecutions genuinely arising from non-political crimes or from acts contrary to the purposes and principles of the United Nations.

Article 15.

(1) Everyone has the right to a nationality.

(2) No one shall be arbitrarily deprived of his nationality nor denied the right to change his nationality.

Article 16.

(1) Men and women of full age, without any limitation due to race, nationality or religion, have the right to marry and to found a family. They are entitled to equal rights as to marriage, during marriage and at its dissolution.

(2) Marriage shall be entered into only with the free and full consent of the intending spouses.

(3) The family is the natural and fundamental group unit of society and is entitled to protection by society and the State.

Article 17.

(1) Everyone has the right to own property alone as well as in association with others.

(2) No one shall be arbitrarily deprived of his property.

Article 18.

Everyone has the right to freedom of thought, conscience and religion; this right includes freedom to change his religion or belief, and freedom, either alone or in community with others and in public or private, to manifest his religion or belief in teaching, practice, worship and observance.

Article 19.

Everyone has the right to freedom of opinion and expression; this right includes freedom to hold opinions without interference and to seek, receive and impart information and ideas through any media and regardless of frontiers.

Article 20.

(1) Everyone has the right to freedom of peaceful assembly and association.

(2) No one may be compelled to belong to an association.

Article 21.

(1) Everyone has the right to take part in the government of his country, directly or through freely chosen representatives.

(2) Everyone has the right of equal access to public service in his country.

(3) The will of the people shall be the basis of the authority of government; this will shall be expressed in periodic and genuine elections which shall be by universal and equal suffrage and shall be held by secret vote or by equivalent free voting procedures.

Article 22.

Everyone, as a member of society, has the right to social security and is entitled to realisation, through national effort and international co-operation and in accordance with the organisation and resources of each State, of the economic, social and cultural rights indispensable for his dignity and the free development of his personality.

Article 23.

(1) Everyone has the right to work, to free choice of employment, to just and favourable conditions of work and to protection against unemployment.

(2) Everyone, without any discrimination, has the right to equal pay for equal work.

(3) Everyone who works has the right to just and favourable remuneration ensuring for himself and his family an existence worthy of human dignity, and supplemented, if necessary, by other means of social protection.

(4) Everyone has the right to form and to join trade unions for the protection of his interests.

Article 24.

Everyone has the right to rest and leisure, including reasonable limitation of working hours and periodic holidays with pay.

Article 25.

(1) Everyone has the right to a standard of living adequate for the health and well-being of himself and of his family, including food, clothing, housing and medical care and necessary social services, and the right to security in the event of unemployment, sickness, disability, widowhood, old age or other lack of livelihood in circumstances beyond his control.

(2) Motherhood and childhood are entitled to special care and

assistance. All children, whether born in or out of wedlock, shall enjoy the same social protection.

Article 26.

(1) Everyone has the right to education. Education shall be free, at least in the elementary and fundamental stages. Elementary education shall be compulsory. Technical and professional education shall be made generally available and higher education shall be equally accessible to all on the basis of merit.

(2) Education shall be directed to the full development of the human personality and to the strengthening of respect for human rights and fundamental freedoms. It shall promote understanding, tolerance and friendship among all nations, racial or religious groups, and shall further the activities of the United Nations for the maintenance of peace.

(3) Parents have a prior right to choose the kind of education that shall be given to their children.

Article 27.

(1) Everyone has the right freely to participate in the cultural life of the community, to enjoy the arts and to share in scientific advancement and its benefits.

(2) Everyone has the right to the protection of the moral and material interests resulting from any scientific, literary or artistic production of which he is the author.

Article 28.

Everyone is entitled to a social and international order in which the rights and freedoms set forth in this Declaration can be fully realised.

Article 29.

(1) Everyone has duties to the community in which alone the free and full development of his personality is possible.

(2) In the exercise of his rights and freedoms, everyone shall be subject only to such limitations as are determined by law solely for the purpose of securing due recognition and respect for the rights and freedoms of others and of meeting the just requirements of morality, public order and the general welfare in a democratic society.

(3) These rights and freedoms may in no case be exercised contrary

to the purposes and principles of the United Nations.

Article 30.

Nothing in this Declaration may be interpreted as implying for any State, group or person any right to engage in any activity or to perform any act aimed at the destruction of any of the rights and freedoms set forth herein.

Adopted on 10th December 1948
by the General Assembly of the United Nations (without dissent)

Appendix II
Refugees and asylum: legal definitions

According to the UN Convention on the Status of Refugees a refugee is someone who has a *'well-founded fear of being persecuted for reasons of race, religion, nationality, membership of a particular social group or political opinion.'* [20] Issues of conflict arise when economic migrants attempt to use the asylum system to gain entry to the European Union. The result has been a controversial tightening up of the legislation surrounding the asylum process throughout the European Union.

The European Convention on Human Rights was adopted by the Council of Europe in 1950 and contains most of the rights contained in the UN Declaration of Human Rights. Among these are the right to life, freedom from slavery, freedom of association, freedom of expression, freedom from torture, protection of privacy and family life, and freedom from discrimination in the application of those rights and freedoms. Applications for asylum often include appeals to the relevant Article in the ECHR in certain circumstances appeals can be addressed to the European Court of Human Rights in Strasbourg. In the UK most of these provisions have been incorporated into domestic law through the Human Rights Act 1998.

Under international law all member countries of the United Nations have an obligation to respect human rights as well as an obligation to enforce them but that is not the case, of course, in dictatorships, one-party states, theocracies and in failed states such as Somalia and Afghanistan.

The UN Convention on the Rights of the Child 1989 has been ratified by every country except in Somalia and the USA and it requires all state institutions – including courts and tribunals – to act *'in the best interests of the child'* (Article 3).

In the European Union refugees are required to apply for asylum in the first place of safety they reach. Under the Dublin Convention, revised in 2003 as the Dublin II Regulations, refugees must apply for asylum in the first EU country they arrive in. Refugees applying in a second country are normally returned to the first country for completion of the process.

In the UK cases are heard before an Adjudicator who may be a judge or someone else with legal training such as a lawyer or academic and they have the power to grant 'permanent leave to remain'. The majority of cases, however, fail at this stage usually on one of two grounds: (i) that the applicant cannot prove they have a 'Convention reason' or (ii) that the applicant cannot prove they would still be in danger if they returned home. The usual phrase that is used of the evidence given, if it is rejected, is that it is 'not credible'.

The problem for asylum seekers is how do you prove to an Adjudicator's satisfaction you were beaten and threatened because of your political activities. There are no witnesses you can call. There is usually no photographic or video evidence. It is simply a matter of your credibility set against the country reports the Adjudicator has to hand.[21] And, similarly, how do you prove there may be dangers for you if you return home? That is often speculative anyway. What refugees have is the *fear* of potential danger but unless that fear is *'well-founded'* it does not constitute legal grounds for not being removed.

Appeals may be lodged but in practice most of these are denied on the basis that the initial decision was correct. A further appeal to the Home Secretary can be lodged. The new but narrow category of Humanitarian Protection aims to offer protection only where it is genuinely required. To be granted Humanitarian Protection, an asylum seeker needs to be at risk from the death penalty, unlawful killing, torture or inhuman or degrading treatment if they were to return to their home country. Those granted refugee status may subsequently apply for citizenship which can take up to 7 years.

In the UK 80,315 asylum applications were received in 2000 of whom 9% were Iraqi Kurds, 8% Sri Lankans, 8% Kosovar Albanians, 7% Iranians and 7% Afghans. In the same year 10,375 applicants received refugee status (11%), 11,495 were given 'exceptional leave to remain' (12%), 75,680 applicants were refused asylum (78%) and only 17% of appeals succeeded (3,340 out of 19,395).[22] By 2003 the number of claims lodged was much reduced as the government sought to 'get on top' of what the tabloids have dubbed the asylum 'problem'.

Wild claims are made about the number of asylum seekers coming into Britain. In the UK there are 1.7 asylum seekers per 1,000 people whereas Armenia has 80, Guinea has 59, and former Yugoslavia has 46.[23] In total Iran has 1.9m refugees and Pakistan has 2 million. They are countries with relatively poor infrastructures and are, therefore, least able to cope. Britain, on the other hand, is a wealthy country with the world's fourth largest economy yet many people still complain we can't cope.

In Britain registered asylum seekers receive only 80% of benefits and they may not work even if they are highly qualified and wish to do so. According to the BBC the annual cost of asylum seekers to the Exchequer in 1999 was £500m. By 2002 it had risen to £1052m. What those figures don't reveal, of course, is the cost to the Exchequer, say, of the estimated one million British people who do not pay their road tax (£200m per year) or the cost of benefit fraud committed by British people (£2 billion per year) or the cost of violent crime as a result of binge drinking (£31.8 billion per year) or the many other scams and crimes committed by UK citizens.[24] Why, therefore, are asylum seekers scapegoated as if they had brought unlawful behaviour into a previously wholly law-abiding country?

Appendix III
Organisations

Addresses and telephone numbers are correct at the time of going to press, in Summer 2004, but please note that websites and email addresses especially are subject to change.

Acorn Healing Trust
Whitehill Chase, Bordon, Hants GU35 OAP
tel 01420-478121
website www.acornchristian.org
or check the following website for other healing centres:
www.fcth.org/allcentres.htm

Action by Christians Against Torture (ACAT-UK)
40 Albert Road, Saltash, Cornwall PL12 4EB
tel 01752-849821
email Lois@acat-uk.freeserve.co.uk

Amnesty International
99-119 Rosebery Avenue, London EC1R 4RE
tel 020-7814-6200
email info@amnesty.org.uk
website www.amnesty.org.uk

Animal Christian Concern
46 St Margaret's Road, Horsforth, Leeds LS18 5BG
tel 0113-258-3517

A Rocha UK (The Rock)
13 Avenue Road, Southall, Middx UB1 3BL
tel 020-8574-5935
email uk@arocha.org
website www. arocha.org

Barnabas Fund
The Old Rectory, River Street, Pewsey, Wiltshire SN9 5DB
tel 01672-564938
fax 01672-565030
email info@barnabasfund.org
website www.barnabasfund.org

Burma Campaign UK
Top Floor, Bickerton House, 25-27 Bickerton Road,
London N19 5JJ
tel 020-7281-7377
website www.burmacampaign.org.uk

Burmese Embassy (Embassy of Myanmar)
His Excellency the Ambassador, 19A Charles Street,
London W1X 8ER
tel 020-7629-4486
(salutation to the Ambassador: Your Excellency)

Burrswood Christian Centre for Medical and Spiritual Care
Burrswood, Groombridge, Tunbridge Wells, Kent TN3 9PY
tel 01892-514112
website www.burrswood.org.uk

Campaign for Nuclear Disarmament (CND and Christian CND)
162 Holloway Road, London N7 8DQ
tel 020-7700-2393
email lionel@cnduk.org
website www.cnduk.org/welcome.htm

Catholic Fund for Overseas Development (CAFOD)
Romero Close, Stockwell Road, London SW9 9TY
tel 020-7733-7900
website www.cafod.org.uk

Chinese Government
Premier Zhu Rongji, Guiwuyuan, 9 Xihuang-chenggen Beijie,
Beijingshi 100032,
People's Republic of China
(salutation to the Premier: Your Excellency)

Chinese Embassy
His Excellency The Ambassador, 49-51 Portland Place,
London W1N 3AH
(salutation to the Ambassador: Your Excellency)

Christian Aid
PO Box 100, London SE1 7RT
tel 020-7620-4444
email info@christian-aid.org
website www.christian-aid.org.uk

Christian Ecology Link
20 Carlton Road, Harrogate HG2 8DD
tel 01423-871616
email info@christian-ecology.org.uk
website www.christian-ecology.org.uk

Christian Solidarity Worldwide
PO Box 99, New Malden, Surrey KT3 3YF
tel 020-8942-8810
website www.csw.org.uk

Church of England
International & Development Affairs Office,
Church House, Great Smith Street, London SW1P 3NZ
tel 020-7898-1533
website www.cofe.anglican.org

Conservative Party
Central Office, 32 Smith Square, London SW1P 3HH
tel 020-7222-9000
website www.conservatives.org

Council for the Advancement of British Arab Understanding
21 Collingham Road, London SW5 ONU
tel 020-7373-8414
email caabu@caabu.org
website www.caabu.org

Council of Churches for Britain & Ireland
Bastille Court, 2 Paris Garden, London SE1 8ND
Tel 020-7654-7254
email info@ctbi.org.uk
website www.ctbi.org.uk

Coventry Cathedral's International Centre for Reconciliation
7 Priory Row, Coventry CV1 5ES
tel 024-7622-7597
website www.coventrycathedral.org

Foreign & Commonwealth Office
King Charles Street, London SW1A 2AH
tel 020-7270-1500
website www.fco.gov.uk

Free Tibet Campaign
1 Rosoman Place, London EC1R OJY
tel 020-77833-9958
website www.freetibet.org

Friends of the Earth
26-28 Underwood Street, London N1 7JQ
tel 020-7490-1555
website www.foe.co.uk

Green Party
1a Waterlow Road, Archway, London N19 5NJ
tel 020-7272-4474
website www.greenparty.org.uk

Greenpeace (UK)
Canonbury Villas, London N1 2PN
tel 020-7865-8100
website www.greenpeace.org.uk

House of Commons (to write to your MP)
London SW1A OAA
email [name.name]@parliament.gov.uk

Iona Community
4th Floor, Savoy House, 140 Sauchiehall Street, Glasgow G2 3DH
tel 0141-332-6343
email ionacomm@gla,iona.org.uk
website www.iona.org.uk

Keston Institute
PO Box 276, Oxford OX2 6BF
tel 01865-792929
email keston.institute@keston.org
website www.keston.org

Labour Party
16 Old Queen Street, London SW1H 9HP
tel 08705-900-200
email info@new.labour.org.uk
website www.labour.org.uk

Liberal Democrats
4 Cowley Street, London SW1P 3NB
tel 020-7222-7999
email info@libdems.org.uk
website www.libdems.org.uk

Liberty
21 Tabard Street, London SE1 4LA
tel 020-7403-3888
website www.liberty-human-rights.org.uk

Plaid Cymru
18 Park Grove, Cardiff CF10 3BN
tel 0292-064-6000
website www.plaidcymru.org

Quakers (The Religious Society of Friends)
Friends House, Euston road, London NW1 2BJ
tel 020-77387-3601
website www.quaker.org.uk

The Refugee Council *(see also the Scottish Refugee Council below)*
3-9 Bondway, London SW8 1SJ
tel 020-7820-3000
website: www.refugeecouncil.org.uk

RSPCA
Causeway, Horsham, West Sussex RH12 1HG
tel 01403-264181
website www.rspca.org.uk

Save the Children Fund
1 St John's Lane, London EC1M 4AR
tel 020 7012 6400 (Volunteer Action Line 0845 606 402)
email supporter.care@savethechildren.org.uk
website www.savethechildren.org.uk

Scottish Catholic International Aid Fund (SCIAF)
5 Oswald Street, Glasgow G1 4QR
tel 0141-221-4447
website www.sciaf.org.uk

Scottish Centre for Non-Violence
Scottish Churches House, Kirk Street, Dunblane,
Perthshire FK15 OAJ
tel 01786-823588
website www.nonviolence-scotland.co.uk

Scottish National Party
6 North Charlotte Street, Edinburgh EH2 4JH
tel 0131-226-3661
website www.snp.org

Scottish Refugee Council
Standard Building, 94 Hope Street, Glasgow G2 6QA
tel 0141-248-9799
website: www.scottishrefugeecounci.org.uk

Scottish Socialist Party
70 Stanley Street, Glasgow, G41 1JB
tel 0141-429-8200
e-mail ssp.glasgow@btinternet.com
website www.scottishsocialistparty.org

United Kingdom Independence Party
123 New John Street, Birmingham B6 4LD
tel 0121-333-7737
e-mail webmail@ukip.org
website www.ukip.org

United Nations Association
3 Whitehall Court, London SW1A 2EL
tel 020-7930-2931
website www.una-uk.org

United Nations Information Centre
21st Floor, Millbank Tower, 21-24 Millbank,
London SW1P 4QP
tel 020-7630-1981
website www.unitednations.org.uk

Permissions

The publishers acknowledge with thanks permission to print the extracts below. Every effort has been made to trace copyright holders; the publishers will gladly rectify any errors or omissions in future editions.

Extract from *No Future without Forgiveness* by Desmond Tutu, published by Rider. Used by permission of the Random House Group Limited.

Extract from *Fire under the Snow* by Palden Gyatso, published by the Harvill Press. Used by permission of the Random House Group Limited.

Extract from *An Evil Cradling* by Brian Keenan, published by Hutchinson. Used by permission of the Random House Group Limited.

Extract from *Strength to Love* by Dr Martin Luther King, reprinted by arrangement with the Estate of Martin Luther King Jr, c/o Writers House LLC as agent for the proprietor, New York, NY, copyright 1958 Martin Luther King Jr., copyright renewed 1986 Coretta Scott King.

Extract from *When Bad Things Happen to Good People* by Harold Kushner, published by Pan Macmillan, used with permission of Macmillan UK.

Extract from *Girlfriend in a Coma* by Douglas Coupland, published by Flamingo/ HarperCollins, latest edition 2004. Used with permission of HarperCollins Publishers Ltd.

Printed in the United Kingdom
by Lightning Source UK Ltd.
101787UKS00002B/79-120